# WAKE UP CALLS

# WAKE UP CALLS

## PRACTICAL INSIGHTS FOR BUSY PEOPLE

# RON HUTCHCRAFT

MOODY PRESS

CHICAGO

*Dedicated to*
*Lisa, Doug, and Brad*

*Your lives honor*
*your Father in heaven*
*and your father on earth.*
*God has used you*
*to teach me so much.*

# A Personal Word...

I resisted radiated ravioli as long as I could. People would talk about how they "nuked" their dinner, and somehow that did not appeal to me.

But our family's wall-to-wall schedule finally convinced me that we sometimes needed instant nutrition. With five busy lives there often isn't time to prepare the meal we need. So although we still like home-cooked, "take time" meals best, we are grateful for a way to eat on the run.

Several years ago, I had to learn to apply "microwave cooking" to *spiritual* food. A radio executive said, "We would like for you to do a program on our station." "Sounds interesting," I replied. "Good," my broadcasting friend answered. "We'll give you five minutes."

Five minutes? My co-workers weren't even sure I could give my *name* in five minutes. Talk about microwave messages!

But today I am deeply grateful for what that five-minute "meal" has taught me. There is life-changing power in a challenge that is brief, biblical, and practical.

So that program, "A Word with You," became a finely sharpened tool. Aired nationally on the Moody Broadcasting Network, these five-minute meals seem to be just what a lot of busy believers need.

Frequently people say, "I was *driving* when you came on. I needed what you said, but I couldn't write it down!" The simple fact is that most people listen to the radio as they eat a meal—on the run. We only *have* five minutes—and often no way to record an insight that really helped us.

So we wrote it down. That's why *Wake Up Calls* was born—to put into retrievable form some of the insights that go by so quickly on radio.

Actually, these brief "visits" are a plateful of focused truth. When you take a glass and focus sunlight on a piece of wood, you can start a little fire with that focused energy. In a similar way spiritual fires can start when we focus *one biblical statement* on *one real-life subject.*

You will find a lot of illustration and analogy here. I learned that from my Master. "Like" seemed to be one of Jesus' favorite words—"My kingdom is *like* this wheat field—*like* this little child—*like* this grapevine." He has taught me that way—by likening unseen heaven-things to familiar earth-things. There's a lot of "like" in these brief chapters.

But the power is not in illustration or brevity—it is packed in the words of God. The Bible is described in Hebrews 4:12 as being "quick and powerful." Now the modern meaning of "quick" is "alive" rather that "fast." Still, I have found the Word of God to be so alive that even a *quick* connection with it can change a day—or a life.

I hope you'll see the Lord Jesus in these pages. And I hope you'll see yourself. The Bible is a mirror (James 1:23-25)—and you usually *change* something after you look in the mirror. Maybe these "mirrors" will help you be a better husband or wife, a better friend or employee, a better parent or manager, a better follower of Christ.

These "microwave meals" are no substitute for the home-cooked food you receive in your personal time with the Lord or your pastor's messages. They *are* instant inspiration for people on the run. And because it is God's high-energy Word, a little can do a lot.

Your "busy" will be "blessed" if you can hear a "wake up call" from Jesus each day.

**Y**ou may be America's biggest baseball card company, but you cannot afford to stand still. Now I wasn't always so knowledgeable about baseball cards, but I have two fanatic collectors in my house, two sons who are pretty good at it. And they have taught me what a huge, multimillion dollar business baseball cards have become. For many years, one company dominated the baseball card scene. In fact, they made the baseball cards when I was a kid, so that goes back to the Fred Flintstone era! But they got a little comfortable as the years went by. Even I could see the difference in the quality. The photos on their cards did not show much action and had little color. They were just the usual boring, head-shots of the players. Needless to say, other companies came along with exciting new designs, photos, and action, and they began to steal a chunk of the big, old company's market. Well, guess what—new cards are now out from the "big, old company," and they look great! The company had learned that when you've been around for a while, you can get careless and complacent and be defeated by a fatal dose of...

## Riding on Your Reputation

Luke 3:3-4, 8 has to do with the ministry of John the Baptist. "He went into all the country around the Jordan, preaching a baptism of repentance for the forgiveness of sins. As is written in the book of the words of Isaiah the prophet: "a voice of one calling in the desert, 'Prepare the way for the Lord, make straight paths for him.' " A great crowd came out to John to be baptized, and he said to them, "Produce fruit in keeping with repentance. And do not begin to say to yourselves, 'We have Abraham as our father,' for I tell you that out of these stones God can raise up children for Abraham" (v. 8). John was saying, "Be ready for His return. Be ready for whenever He calls you home. Be ready for the personal plan He wants to unfold for you."

The way to be ready for Him, according to John the Baptist, is to repent, which literally means "to have a change of mind about sin." A spiritually healthy person is always changing, is always dealing with sinful attitudes and actions that have been pointed out by the Holy Spirit. Just as companies die when they stop changing, so, too, do Christians. John the Baptist confronted the greatest enemy of spiritual growth, spiritual comfort, spiritual position. Some of the people who heard him said to themselves, *We're God's chosen people. We're OK. Our position protects us. We don't have to repent!*

Maybe you, too, have been around long enough to close your eyes to your need to change, to root out sin, to repent. You see, the two sentences "I'm a big deal" and "I need to change" don't often go together. Out of the very stones of the earth God could make a preacher, a teacher, an elder, a radio preacher, a spiritual celebrity, an officer in the church, a person in leadership. God is not impressed with these positions. He is impressed with whether or not you are dealing with the sin in your life. The older you get in Christ and the more influence you have in His Kingdom, the more tempted you will be to tolerate sin in your life. "So many people think I'm OK, I guess I must be." Each of us should pray, "Lord, shake me up! Don't let me settle for mediocrity."

A baseball card company rode on its reputation and fell asleep. It could happen to you—if reputation replaces repentance. *What change will you make today* because of Jesus?

**A**few days ago, our family had a memorable experience. We went for a sleigh ride in "a one-horse open sleigh," jingle bells and all. As we rode along, my wife asked the old Vermonter who was driving the sleigh, "Why do they have these jingle bells?" He told her that the bells were developed to keep the horses calm. What? "Yes," the driver said. "The sounds of the sleigh and the people in the sleigh can make a horse skittish and ready to bolt, or run, or rear back. A lot of times when the horses are on hard, crunchy snow as the sleigh starts up, the sound of the sleigh frightens them and can really cause problems. So, they developed "jingle bells," to keep the horses soothed by the gentle rhythm of their sound. When the horse hears the bells "other sounds don't bother him." People are sort of like that, too. If we can hear a reassuring voice we are used to, we can relax. There is, in fact, an important connection between...

# Jingle Bells and Wedding Bells

First Peter 3:7 is a verse about marriage, specifically about the way husbands deal with their wives. Now I'm going to have to be careful here, because the analogy I'm developing might make it sound like I'm comparing a wife to a horse. That is not my intent. What I'm talking about is the similarity of the bells on the sleigh to the sound of a voice a person can trust. First Peter 3:7 says, "Husbands, in the same way be considerate as you live with your wives, and treat them with respect as the weaker partner and as heirs with you of the gracious gift of life, so that nothing will hinder your prayers." You might ask, what does that have to do with jingle

12

bells? Well, we're talking here about the steady, predictable, consistent attention of a husband for his wife. In the one-horse open sleigh, jingle bells are the rhythm that stabilizes a horse's run and lets him know that he can relax. There's an important biblical principle here. It is that a husband's consistent attention and availability stabilizes a woman's heart and life. I don't think my wife is that different from yours. I know that she's running hard most of the time with deadlines and demands and supporting all of our busy lives with everything she can give. When she can count on regular time with me she can handle those pressures. But she cannot handle them as well when I'm unavailable, for we are built to need each other.

Is your voice, your attention, a dependable rhythm in your wife's life? Or are you too busy to listen to her or to guarantee her regular time together? Is everyone else getting your best, and your wife getting your leftovers? Give your wife the royal treatment the Bible commands. Give her prime time. If you don't, you'll notice a negative result. There will be fear, panic, resentment. She may even become a nag—and all because she does not have the attention she needs to be able to count on. If you've heard the wedding bells, then learn from the jingle bells. Put your wife first. Be the dependable rhythm that lets her know that everything is OK.

13

**T**upperware is a great invention. I just wish the tops were attached permanently to the containers. I don't know if you have this problem, but somehow the tops and the containers always seem to get separated, and we're scrounging around in the bottom of some cupboard trying to find a top for the crazy thing! But I refuse to put good food in the refrigerator without a top on the Tupperware. You see, when something is left open in the refrigerator, it starts to collect the odor—the flavor—of everything else that's there. If you want to keep the flavor of the food you place in the refrigerator, you have to keep it covered. Otherwise it will pick up smells and tastes that can ruin the flavor. It will have absorbed the odors of its surroundings. Spoilage is the result when something keeps...

## Collecting Odors

In Ephesians 5:1, 8*b*-11 Paul gives positive and negative admonition. "Be imitators of God, therefore, as dearly loved children, and live a life of love," he says (v. 1). "Live as children of the light...and find out what pleases the Lord" (vv. 8*b*, 10). That's the way we are meant to live. Now for the negative. "Have nothing to do with the fruitless deeds of darkness, but rather expose them" (v. 11). If you allow yourself to be exposed to what's dirty or what's dark, what's angry or mean, you will—without knowing it—start tasting like your surroundings. You will start collecting odors. Some of those "odors," or works of darkness, are.listed in verses 3 and 4. "There must not be even a hint of sexual immorality, or of any kind of impurity, or of greed....Nor should there be obscenity, foolish talk or coarse joking."

It may be that you've allowed yourself to be around what's evil. You're not into it, but you're around it. Slowly, but surely, you're being poisoned. You haven't noticed it yet, but you're harder than you used to be. You're not soft and gentle. You're starting to laugh at things that break God's heart. You are experiencing more wrong thinking about the opposite sex than you used to. Your interest in God's Word has gone down, and your interest in what's worldly has gone up. It's a slow, subtle process—but it's deadly. That's because the devil doesn't destroy a Christian by explosion—he does it by erosion. He slowly wears you down and infects you with the attitudes and thoughts that will set you up for a fall.

The Bible says, "Have nothing to do with the fruitless deeds of darkness" (v. 11). That doesn't mean you should isolate yourself and refuse to be with people who need Christ. No, it is instead a commitment to turn your back on sin in any form. It's a commitment to turn to a new TV channel rather that watch to see how bad the program's going to be. It's a commitment to control the creeping invasion of sin-suggesting music into your mind. It's a commitment to turn down invitations to places you know are going to wear you down. You are royalty. You are too special to wallow in junk! Have you been open—too open—to the humor, the music, and the empty talk that characterizes the darkness around you? Maybe you're collecting odors. Before you're spoiled, put a lid on it!

**Y**ou can tell that kids think they're unbreakable by the risks they take. They'll jump off, or into, almost anything. They drive as though they are immortal. They try all kinds of crazy stunts and pranks as though they are indestructible. We, too, do that. We live as though the bad things will always happen to someone else. We know better, we know we're not indestructible, but we live as if we're unbreakable, as if we've got all the time in the world. But we don't. Time is moving inexorably forward even though...

# We Cannot See the Clock

Proverbs 21:1 and Ephesians 5:16 deal with the elements of time and opportunity. Proverbs 27:1 says, "Do not boast about tomorrow, for you do not know what a day may bring forth." In other words, we don't know how late it is. It's as though we were placed in a room and given a large task to do but not been told how much time we had to do it in or even what time it is. The clock has been covered, or perhaps it has been placed behind our backs or on a shelf out of sight. None of us knows how much time is left on our own personal clock.

When I was thirty-three it seemed to me I had most of my life to live. Then a friend died of a heart attack. Suddenly I realized that I didn't actually know how much time I had left. My friend was only thirty-three. A friend of ours has a similar tale. One day a seventeen-year old friend of his began to complain of symptoms that were severe enough to make him seek out the care of a doctor. The doctor said, "I think that it's the flu going around." so the young man went to bed and slept—and began to get worse. By eleven o'clock that night, he was dead of spinal meningitis. Thank God this seventeen-year old young man was a Christian and ready to meet his Lord. But if you had asked him the day before what his prospects for a long life were, I am sure he would have told you he had most of his days yet to live. But he couldn't see the clock.

Tomorrow is not guaranteed. We should not count on it. When we think we have a great deal of something, we are likely to use it carelessly. That's what happens with the days we have been given. We say to ourselves, *I've got plenty of days*. But we don't *know* that we do. Each day is therefore too precious to waste.

God's life-style is summed up in Ephesians 5:16: "[Make] the most of every opportunity." The King James Version says, "Redeem the time." *The Amplified Bible* reads, "Buy up each opportunity—because the days are evil." Many of us have thought we had plenty of time to get things done. Surely, we think, there will be time enough to say, "I love you," and, "I appreciate you" to the people around us. Then, suddenly, we find that our time is up. *I've got time to make things right with my friend*, we say to ourselves. Then that person with whom you never made it right is gone, and you have the scar for a lifetime. *I'll come to Christ someday*, we think, and then we have waited one day too long. *I'll give my family time, I really will! I just need to get past some of these busy years*. Then, suddenly, it's too late. *I'll start serving the Lord*, we promise. But while we've waited, lives have slipped by forever. What if your total contribution on earth was your life up to today? That might be all you get, you know. Dedicate each day to the Lord. Live wholeheartedly. Don't hold back if God is telling you to do something. If you're ever going to do it, do it now! Life is too short to waste a day! We don't know how much time is left—we can't see the clock—so let's make this day an investment in eternity!

**A**s 1986 ended, television and print commentators were looking back at the greatest—and the most tragic—moments of the year. They all mentioned Len Bias—twenty-two years old, the number one college basketball star in the United States, and drafted by the Boston Celtics. He had signed a $1.6 million contract to do commercials. *Newsweek* magazine said of him, "[These] were the best days of his life." And so he went to celebrate in a dorm at the University of Maryland, snorted some cocaine, and kept using it. His friends warned him. "Be careful," they said. And he is reported to have replied, "I can handle anything." He was dead within hours.

In a sense, success killed him. And that is true of many persons. Many an athletic team has won a lop-sided, easy victory one week, only to give away in the next game to an embarrassing defeat. In some ways, we are all never in greater danger than when we are on a roll. You, too, could be a victim of...

## The Dangers of Winning

Our word for today comes from 2 Chronicles 26:3-16. the Scripture text is about a man who was "on a roll," a man who was winning. He was one of the kings—for a while, one of the *great* kings—of the Old Testament. Second Chronicles 26:3 introduces him: "Uzziah was sixteen years old when he became king, and he reigned in Jerusalem fifty-two years." A later verse describes the first part of his reign: "As long as he sought the Lord, God gave him success" (v. 5*b*). the chapter then tells of the armies he defeated, the buildings and towers he built, the army he raised. "His fame spread far and wide," it says, "for he was greatly helped" (v. 15*b*). But then the word *until* appears. Uzziah "was greatly helped until he became powerful" (v. 15*c*). The Scripture is forthright in its assessment: "After Uzziah became powerful, his pride led to his downfall. He was unfaithful to the Lord his God" (v. 16*a*). Here he was at first: young, struggling, unsure, but dependent on the Lord. There was a little of him and a lot of God. Then, suddenly, after all those years, he was on top. Now there was a lot of him and only a little of God. In the hard times, you know you need the Lord, you pray desperately, you trust Him just to get you through the day. But then the good times arrive. You're a success in business and romantically, the finances are finally there, things have come around—and great! Enjoy it! But don't lose your childlike dependency on the Lord who brought you there, or you won't be there for long.

Has the Lord been hearing less from you since things got better? If your success makes you more self-centered, less Christ-centered, it could be the worst thing that ever happened to you. Each day, acknowledge the Lord as the author of your success. It is not your achievement—it is His gift. You've never needed Him more! That's because God can trust success only to those who continually stay close to Him even when they're winning. God has trusted *you* with good times for the present. Do ont betray that trust.

If you forget who brought you this winning season, it could quickly turn into a losing season.

**G**uards. That's a good way to recognize the places folks think are important. For example, we obviously think the White House is important—there are guards all around it. The bank usually has a guard. There are some club communities in our area where you aren't even allowed into the neighborhood until the guard says, "Yes, somebody left your name at the booth. You can go in." There are guards at the airport, at military installations, and even at the ballpark. Important places need to be guarded.

But it's not just banks and ballparks that need guarding. There is a place inside your life that needs a guard—and yet it probably doesn't have one. That's not because of what will get in, though. It's because of what can get out. You really should secure this location because...

# A Guard Can Spare You Grief

Proverbs 13:3; 21:23, 28; and Romans 3:10-18 have to do with a part of your body that may be doing you a good deal of damage and that needs a guard—because important places have guards. Proverbs 13:3 says, "He who guards his lips guards his life, but he who speaks rashly will come to ruin." A few chapters later, Proverbs 21:23 says, "He who guards his mouth and his tongue keeps himself from calamity." God is talking here about a lip-guard. (Is that a product? It should be.) We need a lip-guard. Romans 3 tells us that "there is no one righteous, not even one" (v. 10). In describing our sinfulness as human beings, Romans 3:10-18 gives the anatomy of sin. Our eyes, our feet, and our mouth are involved, the latter mentioned four times. The emphasis suggests that most of the sinning we do, we do with our mouths.

Did you let go something verbal today? Maybe those words hurt another person, or your reputation, or your chance to get something you need or want. Maybe they hurt the reputation of Jesus Christ. The sins of the mouth are the most common and the most damaging, and—sadly—the most accepted. But they shouldn't be. When you let Christ become the Lord of your lips and the Master of your mouth, you are really getting serious about your faith. Proverbs links this matter to survival. Paraphrased, it says, "Guard your lips—it's like guarding your life" (see 21:23, 28). It's for your own good. But somehow there's that last word you had to have, that seemed so clever—the sarcasm, the epithet, the accusation, the put-down. If only we could erase words the way we erase a recording, or the scars the way we erase chalk—but we can't.

We need a lip-guard. It's time to focus the transforming power of the Holy Spirit on our runaway lips. It's got to be a daily battle and one joined early. Before you speak to anyone, consecrate your mouth to the Lord. Ask for grace to pause before you shoot someone verbally. Then start enjoying some victories. Rejoice that there are things that almost were said, but you thought about them, prayed about them, and never spoke them. Don't let your mouth run on as it has been doing. Ask your Lord to guard your mouth. After all, important places have a guard, and nothing you have has more effect than your mouth. Your lip-guard should never go off duty.

**T**he first time I flew into New York City, the man who picked me up said, "Well, you just landed on the garbage of New York."

"What do you mean by that?" I asked.

"Well," he replied, "LaGuardia Airport is built on land-fill. Years ago, garbage trucks hauled the garbage of New York City out here and built a place where there is now an airport."

I was impressed. It's amazing what engineers can do. They had made something very useful out of garbage—just like the Engineer who designed you and me. In fact, one of God's most impressive miracles is...

# Recyclying Garbage

Psalm 51 is a deeply moving psalm because of the point in David's life when he wrote it. David had sinned the great sin of adultery with Bathsheba and had engineered the murder of her husband at the battlefront. As the psalm opens he is groping his way back to the Lord, repenting and seeking forgiveness. If I were to title the psalm, I would call it "David at the Dump," because he was really facing a garbage situation—the garbage of his life. Listen to excerpts from the psalm: "Wash away all my iniquity and cleanse me from my sin....Let me hear joy and gladness; let the bones you have crushed rejoice....Create in me a pure heart, O God, and renew a steadfast spirit within me....Restore to me the joy of your salvation....Then I will teach transgressors your ways, and sinners will turn back to you" (vv. 2-13). David knew where to begin cleaning up the garbage of his life. He knew he had to acknowledge its ugliness, and that he did. Then he said, in effect, "Lord, I'm counting on You. Please, clean it up. Give me a new kind of purity. And then give me a determined, a steadfast spirit. I've learned from this. I'm not going to make these mistakes again. Please give me back my joy better than ever." Notice the result he envisioned. "God is going to make the garbage in my life a source of ministry! I will teach transgressors Your ways, and sinners will turn back to You."

It's an exciting concept—to recognize that God can take the garbage of a sin-scarred life and turn it into credentials of His grace. The same thing happened to the apostle Paul. As Saul of Tarsus he murdered and imprisoned Christians, but when he became converted that violent past was the means of opening many doors. When he came to people with the gospel they asked in surprise, "You're a follower of Christ?!" People could see that Christ really could change a man's life. Paul's past was turned into something very useful.

How many times I've heard people say, "You know after all I've been through, though I would not want to endure it again, I know that experience has given me a unique ability to help people who are where I was." Maybe you've been the victim of sin. I think of Leslie, who was abused by her father but through Christ resolved that relationship and learned to forgive and love him. She is having a powerful ministry now among people who were sinned against in the same way. This is not to encourage anyone to play in garbage. It is far better never to have been there. It is to say that if there is garbage in your past, bring it to the Lord Jesus, to the cross, where He paid for it all. Let Him forgive you and clean you up. And most miraculously, let Him use it for His glory. The power of Christ is so great that it reaches even to the garbage dumps of our lives and turns trash into treasure.

Each of us has his favorite ice cream store. Now I have no commercial interest in this and no stock in Baskin Robbins, but frankly, I must admit that that's the place I like to go most. They have so many flavors! I don't know anybody else who has more. Or maybe it only seems they have more flavors because they have such unique flavors. They call them things I've never heard before. It takes me a while to decide which one I want, but the variety is the fun.

Can you imagine an ice cream store that offered only vanilla? How boring! After a while, you would get tired of the same old flavor. Can you imagine someone's saying, "I only eat vanilla. Never tried anything else." I'd say to him, "Hey, look at the list! You're missing so much." You could have ice cream in many different ways.

Your life will be much more exciting when you learn to appreciate God's...

## So Many Flavors

In 1 Corinthians 12 we go to God's "ice cream parlor," the church, the Body of Christ. Notice the many flavors: "There are different kinds of gifts, but the same Spirit. There are different kinds of service, but the same Lord. There are different kinds of working, but the same God works all of them in all men" (vv. 4-6). Verse 12 says, "The body is a unit, though it is made up of many parts; and though all its parts are many, they form one body. So it is with Christ." If we could take only one message from these wonderful verses, we would be well served if it was this: variety is God's plan for His Body. He is not interested in "cookie-cutter" Christians. He wants many styles—yes, many flavors—of Christians. God likes variety.

We like uniformity. We want everybody to be like us. As a consequence, generally speaking, Baptist Christians know only Baptist Christians; Assembly of God Christians know only Assembly of God Christians; Christian Reformed Christians only Christian Reformed Christians; Presbyterian Christians know only Presbyterian Christians; and on and on. Yet none of us individually has all of Him, though all of us together do have all of Him.

Don't cut yourself off from the other flavors. Don't be a "vanilla Christian." Keep in mind that the various Christian groups disagree on only about 10 percent of Christian doctrine. They agree on 90 percent of Christian teaching concerning Christ, sin, salvation, Christ's return, and the Bible. Christians need on another. Different styles and different emphases in the body of Christ are not only part of God's will, they make you rich. One group of Christians may teach you how to pray. Another group may have a vision for missions and help you care about a lost world. Others may focus on personal evangelism. Still other groups of Christians can help you learn more about God's sovereign control over things. One group may be strong, loving, and caring. Another may be particularly effective in worship or in careful Bible study. We Christians will be together forever. Why not begin *now* to get together? Whenever you're against what divides His Body, you're on God's side. It's not all vanilla! There are lots of flavors, but it's all ice cream. Don't limit the work of God to the flavor you like best. He has so many flavors!

**C**ertain birthdays are more important than others. Take a fortieth birthday. We have set apart that particular birthday as a special milestone. I remember that when my wife, Karen, reached her fortieth birthday she handled it very well. It was no big deal. It wasn't as though some great river had been crossed in her life—that is, until a couple of months later, when our then-twelve-year old son said to her, "Hey, Mom, do you know you've been on earth for 14,662 days?!"

Well, when you put it that way, it took on a whole new outlook. Forty years doesn't sound bad, but fourteen thousand plus days? That was different story.

What our son said got us to thinking about the days we had had with our three children—and how many of those days were gone. How quickly they had slipped away. It gave us a new look at the days we still had. With time disappearing so quickly, we need to be...

# Capturing Days

Ephesians 5:15-17 reads, "Be very careful, then, how you live—not as unwise but as wise, making the most of every opportunity, because the days are evil. Therefore do not be foolish, but understand what the Lord's will is." Now the verse in the middle of the passage, verse 16, talks about "making the most of every opportunity." It's sandwiched between two intriguing admonitions—don't live unwisely (in other words, live smart) and don't be foolish. Then the passage talks about our destiny and the need to understand God's will. But the key thought is "making the most of every opportunity." You want to "live smart," to do God's will? Then seize every opportunity!

It's no coincidence that the verses that follow this exhortation are about family relationships. In 6:4 Paul has this to say to fathers: "Bring...up [your children] in the training and instruction of the Lord." How do you do that? You do it by capturing each twenty-four hour period as another moment to mold the lives of your children and your grandchildren. You will have little time to strengthen them for a world that is lost. Ask yourselves, *Have we touched the Lord together with our children? Have we talked about where we saw Him in our lives today? Have we celebrated how something in the Bible proved true today? Have we prayed about something real and personal together? Or explored the Bible together? Have we touched each other today? Have we expressed love and affection? Have we got in touch with what made each other happy today—and what hurt?*

The greatest classroom our kids will ever experience is the classroom of everyday life, the natural teaching that is in the flow of the day. You see, by the time you finally have time for formal periods of instruction with your kids, they probably won't. One of the greatest burdens of my life is that we lost so many days. One of the greatest challenges of my life is to make the most of the days ahead. I means that I have had to reorder some priorities, carving out time in what often is a wall-to-wall schedule, and asking God each morning for the opportunities, the determination, the timing to mark my children for Christ that day. The days are flying by. Let us grasp each one and capture it for Christ.

It has probably been a long time since you've asked someone, "How's your liver today?" I never even thought about a liver until my wife, Karen, got sick. She had hepatitis, and for many months I learned how vital the liver is. It's the filtration plant of your body. Each day all kinds of toxic materials are pumping into us—part of the medicines we take and foods we eat—and the liver keeps those poisons from entering the bloodstream. So liver diseases such as hepatitis or cirrhosis can cripple or even kill you, if the poison can't be filtered.

There is another failure of the filtration that in its sphere is equally deadly. But it doesn't have anything to do with a liver. This filtration failure threatens a person with...

# Poison in the Bloodstream

Matthew 27:18 has to do with one of history's most ironic and tragic episodes. Israel's Messiah has come in the Person of Jesus Christ, and yet ironically, the religious leaders are clamoring to have Him executed. They bring Him to Pilate, because they don't have independent authority to put Him to death. At this point in Matthew, when Jesus is on trial before Pilate, a sobering footnote, as it were, appears. It's a kind of spiritual EKG that looks inside the human heart, looks at what makes a person mean, critical, and destructive. It identifies a poison in the heart. Here's what the text says: "For [Pilate] knew it was out of envy that they had handed Jesus over to him." The King James puts it this way: "For he [Pilate] knew that for envy they had delivered [Jesus up to him]." Now the accusers of Jesus covered their motives with a smoke screen. They gave other reasons for what they were doing, and most of it was spiritual talk. There were religious reasons, they said, for their opposition to Jesus. They sounded very, very spiritual about it. But the real issue, the bottom line, was envy. Jesus was delivered up because of it.

People are still being delivered up because of envy. *Webster's* defines envy as "painful or resentful awareness of an advantage enjoyed by another joined with a desire to possess the same advantage, or success." Envy is a denial of God's faithful provision for His children. It's saying, "Hey, how come he's got one? How come I can't have any?" Often it causes us to crucify people—with religious words, of course.

Envy is a poison in the bloodstream. It always starts with comparing. You can't envy unless first you compare homes, or children, or opportunities, or clothes, or positions. Think of someone you've been critical of lately, maybe negative toward, or of someone you start getting dark feelings toward when he comes around. Examine your motives honestly. Could there be envy at the root? You've seen what you perceive to be a position of superiority, or some kind of advantage, or his apparent success. Ask yourself, *If envy is in my life, who is the most likely object of it?* Envy gets all dressed up and starts to deliver someone for destruction. It's an ugly poison. Pray for the person you envy and call envy by name. Trust your Shepherd to give you what is right for you. Filter out the poison of envy. It's a killer.

**W**hen a bridge collapses, it's always inconvenient. And sometimes it's tragic. Several years ago, a bridge on the thruway near Albany, New York, collapsed under the pressure of heavy floodwaters, and several vehicles plunged into a raging river, taking their occupants to their deaths. It isn't always that tragic. But whenever a bridge is out, it makes it much more difficult to get from one point to another. In fact, sometimes the bridge is the only way to get there. Sometimes the bridge is a person. And lives can be lost because of...

# The Collapse of a Two-Legged Bridge

In 2 Corinthians 5:19b-20 the apostle Paul writes, "He [God] has committed to us the ministry of reconciliation. We are therefore Christ's ambassadors, as though God were making his appeal through us. We implore you on Christ's behalf: Be reconciled to God." When I read those verses, I get a mental picture of a great chasm. On one side is Jesus; on the other side, close to me, is someone who does not yet know Christ, as far as I know. Is there such a person in *your* life? Think about him. Maybe he lives right near you. Maybe you drive by his home all the time, or walk past. Maybe he works near you or goes to school with you. Perhaps he is someone you talk with on the phone a lot, possibly a family member, or someone in your carpool. The word I want to stress here is the word *reconciliation*. God has committed to us the message and the ministry of reconciliation. That means there needs to be a bridge over the chasm that separates that person from Jesus. Guess who the bridge is? The bridge is *you*. Is that person moving toward Jesus because of you? Or is he as far from Him as he's ever been? Is it possible that his bridge to Jesus has collapsed?

Sometimes the bridge collapses because we are so busy. *I have so many things to do with my life, I can never get around to talking to him about Christ,* we think. Then the days become weeks, and the weeks become months, and the months become years, and the years become never—and the opportunity is lost. Sometimes it's fear. But your greatest fear should not be of rejection, it should be fear that the person you care about will be lost forever. Sometimes it's the kind of peer pressure that makes you start doing things that lead your friend to wonder if being a Christian is really all that different from not being one. When I was a freshman in college, I woke up one morning to the news that a girl I had gone to high school with had been murdered. Like me, she was a college freshman. I thought back over all the conversations we had had about everything but Christ. I was the bridge, and I had collapsed for her.

I can't help but wonder if somewhere in the corners of eternity, someone we knew on earth won't cry out to us, "Why didn't you tell me? We talked about everything. Why didn't you tell me about Christ?" Listen, there's still time—not for the person who has already gone into eternity but certainly for the people you know now. Jesus is standing on one side with outstretched arms. The person you care about is on the other—restless and lost until he is on Jesus' side. All he needs is a bridge. You are that bridge.

**I**f you're paying attention, your children will tip you off early in their lives as to what to expect from them later on. We have movies of our daughter Lisa, for example, when she was, five, six, seven years old, singing for us, using a spoon—a big, wooden spoon—as a microphone and standing on something in the living room as a stage. That was a tip off to the musical ministry she now has as a young adult.

When my son Brad was five, he was tying our house together with string—very imaginatively. I would walk up to the house and open the back door—and the drawer of my dresser in the bedroom would open. He had everything tied together. Sure enough, as a teenager he's the technician of the family. He loves to figure out how things work, how to take them apart, and—we hope—how to put them together and to solve problems. There is a pattern, a connective line, from the past to the future in the life of every child—my child, God's child. And you can trace...

## *The Leading of a Lifetime*

Verse 4 of Psalm 37 says, "Delight yourself in the Lord and he will give you the desires of your heart. Commit your way to the Lord; trust in Him and He will do this: He will make your righteousness shine like the dawn, the justice of your case like the noonday sun." Verse 23 says, "The steps of a good man are ordered by the Lord: and he delighteth in His way" (KJV*). Don't you get the feeling as you hear in these verses about how God leads that His leading in our lives is a consistent, long-term pattern? It

32

usually is not some sudden departure. Rather, God leads in a straight and consistent line from the past, through the present, and into the future.

You may be at a crossroads right now. It may be a time of decision for you, a time for a major choice. One guideline in determining what God wants for you in the future is to see where He has led you in the past. Psalm 37:4 talks about the Lord's giving you the desires of your heart. Could you trust *your* desires in this decision? If you have kept the first part of the verse, "Delight yourself in the Lord," you probably could. Over the last months and years have you been having a daily time with the Lord, where you were enjoying Him? Then "commit your way to the Lord," as the psalm puts it. Say, in effect, "Lord, anything goes. Whatever you say is OK." With your commitment to and delight in the Lord in mind, when you are trying to decide the path to take, look at the desires you have felt for a long time, not just for days. And if those desires line up with God's Word, and good counsel, and the facts, those desires are probably God-planted.

Keep a spiritual diary of what the Lord says to you through the Bible. Don't make a major decision on the basis of one verse, but look at the things God has been saying to you over and over. Look for the pattern. God's will for tomorrow will put together all He's been doing in your life up to the present—the experiences, the fulfilling achievements, the talents, the desires, the themes He has unfolded for you in His Word. Before you look ahead, look back at God's pattern in your life. His will is the natural next step of following Him daily. He's leading you in a straight line. Don't just grab the impulse of the moment. Look for the leading of a lifetime.

*King James Version.

**W**hen we graduate from childhood to "grown-up-hood," we trade in simple games for complicated ones. Once we get bigger, we learn the rules of football, baseball, and basketball—and they can get pretty complicated. But when you were little you played uncomplicated games. My favorite was dive-bomber. It had simple rules. All you had to do was come in with your arm extended and knock the hat off the other guy's head. That was not too complicated. Keep-away was simple too—just throw the ball back and forth, keeping it away from the guy in the middle. That was easy. So was dodgeball. When another guy tried to throw the ball at you, you tried to dodge it! We boys got pretty good at dodging. Some still are. And that's unfortunate because...

## Catching Beats Dodging

Genesis 3:7-10 introduces us to an interesting and frustrating trait in a man—especially if you happen to be a woman. It's a trait that goes way back—all the way back! Listen to what happened. Adam and Eve having sinned in the Garden of Eden, their "eyes...were opened, and they realized they were naked; so they sewed fig leaves together and made coverings for themselves. Then the man and his wife heard the sound of the Lord God as He was walking in the garden in the cool of the day, and they hid from the Lord God among the trees of the garden. But the Lord God called to the man, 'Where are you?'

"He answered, 'I heard you in the garden, and I was afraid because I was naked. So I hid.' "

It is interesting. When God came to talk with Adam and Eve after that first sin, Adam grabbed Eve's hand and ran and hid! And he is still running. Running from substantial converstation. Running from confrontation. Running from talking with Eve. When it comes to conversations about feelings, personal or interpersonal problems, or conflicts, the male of the species is the great postponer.

A wife says, "Honey, we need to talk." So the husband turns out the light, or he says, "Later, baby." A child is showing signs of needing strong guidance, or direction, and Dad will put off confronting the issue as long as possible, sometimes until there is a heart-wrenching crisis. Men tend to avoid areas where they're not sure of their competence. So they talk about activities, achievements, sports, and politics. Many men are unsure of themselves when it comes to deeply personal areas. So they play dodgeball. Those personal problems build up until they explode!

As a man, I must resist the urge to run, to postpone, to say "later" when it comes to significant conversation. Many tragedies would have been averted if only a man hadn't put off dealing with problems, hadn't let the sun go down on a conflict. If we are to be the leaders God has commanded us to be, we've got to face issues, discuss deep feelings, and solve problems while they are small enough to solve. It is far more manly to catch the challenge thrown at us than to dodge it!

**I** went out shooting with a friend of mine a while back, and I got a high-caliber scare, because the report of one volley of gun-fire was so loud it momentarily made me deaf. Even though it lasted only a few minutes, it was all the deafness I ever want to experience. It was not pleasant to face the prospect of never again hearing a child's laughter, tender words, music, or a bird's singing, and it gave me a new understanding of the tragedy of deafness. But not all deafness is a tragedy. One kind is a triumph. In fact, life can actually be enriched by...

## *Planned Deafness*

Psalm 46 is a very familiar passage of the Bible. David proclaims at the beginning of the psalm that "God is our refuge and strength, an ever-present help in trouble" (v. 1). Then he declares, "We will not fear, though the earth give way and the mountains fall into the heart of the sea, though the waters roar and foam and the mountains quake with their surging" (vv. 2-3). God's message to us in times of upheaval, the psalmist reports, is definite: "Be still and know that I am God" (v. 10).

In the earlier part of his career the great Bible scholar William Barclay was a magnificent preacher. Then he realized that he was going deaf. Finally, he became almost totally deaf. Instead of losing hope, he consecrated this new life of deafness to the Lord. He immersed himself in a world where he could hear only one voice—the voice of God. That environment opened up new understandings that have enriched thousands of people through the many commentaries Barclay penned.

It is God's intention that we have times of planned deafness, times when we are deaf to every other voice but His. Jesus often observed such times, even in the midst of the most demanding responsibilities. God made us in such a way that we need regular time where we hear no voice but His.

That requires privacy. You have to find a place to be alone with God. It requires a block of time, because it takes more than a few minutes to silence the chatter inside, so that you hear only one voice. It requires consistency. Practice makes perfect. You need to build one day on another.

The poet Emily Dickinson said in one of her poems, "The world is too much with us." Do you ever feel like that? Well, when it's your time to hear only one voice, turn off the radio, the Walkman, the phone. Turn away even from those closest to you and get in touch with heaven. Some things that looked big will look smaller. You will experience a shower for your soul that will wash off the stresses of living. But it won't happen unless you plan it! Plan to be deaf to earth for a while—so that you can hear from heaven!

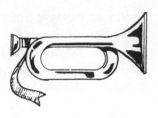

I n recent years, one four-letter word has come to strike terror in the human heart. *Jaws*. Just think how you feel when you hear the word. Well, the jaws I have in mind now are not the kind an orthodontist repairs. No, I have in mind the jaws of that terrorist of the sea, the shark. Sharks are pretty nasty fellows. Consider what attracts them—blood. When someone is wounded, they move in for the kill. Where there's bleeding, there are sharks. In fact, we are all victims—and victimizers—in a cycle called...

# The Shark Syndrome

Not all sharks are in the ocean. Some "sharks" prey on the frailty of the human spirit. We're talking about wounds, about people who hurt you, about tense relationships—and we have healing wisdom from the Scriptures. Proverbs 17:9 provides down-home wisdom on the subject of sharks. "He who covers an offense, promotes love, but whoever repeats a matter separates close friends." Notice the two approaches. One is to "repeat the matter." The other is to "cover the offense." Now, in "shark-talk" you can pounce on the offense, or you can swim on by. Depending on which you do, one of two outcomes will prevail. If you pounce on that hurt—that wound, that problem, that hurt that's been inflicted on you—the result will be separated friends. If you choose to overlook the matter, love will be promoted. It all depends on whether you want to be an overlooker or a scorekeeper. You see, if you love someone, you can swim by all kinds of hurts and problems. You can say, "Well, yeah, but I love him. I can forget it." If you don't love someone, you don't forget *anything* he does wrong! You remember—and replay—every infraction. That's how marriages are torn down, that's how parents and children come apart, and that's how friendships are ruined and working partners become enemies. Christ's love is not some sticky-sweet emotional syrup. It's practical. Without it, we become selective recorders, recording the data that proves that person is as bad as we said—recording the wounds. But real love lets all kinds of hurts go by. A relationship of yours might be suffering from your overly efficient memory. You've been remembering, adding up offenses, keeping score, and attacking where there's a wound. Here's a good prayer for today, "Dear Lord, teach me to be an overlooker." Don't add up the hurts and the wounds. Let it go. Who needs any more sharks? Swim on by!

**B**ecause some of my work is with high school athletes, I have a really special privilege. I get to spend a lot of time in locker rooms. Now, there's something very distinctive about the aroma of a locker room. It is, as the kids say, gross! I don't think there will ever be a best-selling fragrance called "Essence of Locker Room." Athletes carry into that room all the accumulated odors of sweat and dirt from their exercises. Fortunately, they leave those odors there—if they get a shower every day, which they'd better. Our daily lives are just that. Regular "showers" are essential when you're…

# Living in a Locker Room

In John 15:3 Jesus says, "You are already clean because of the Word I have spoken to you." That is a simple but profound statement. Jesus is talking about the cleansing power of the Bible, God's Word. The concept appears also in Ephesians 5, in the great passage on marriage (vv. 22-33). There Paul enjoins husbands to "love [their] wives, just as Christ loved the church and gave himself up for her" (v. 25). Christ "gave himself up" for the church in order "to make her holy, cleansing her by the washing with water through the word" (v. 26). We are the church—we who believe in Christ. The Bible gives us a "brain washing." And our brain *needs* to be washed, for we live in a locker room! Each day we are bombarded with tons of dirt. We hear gross talk and foul language—so frequently, in fact, we almost don't even notice it anymore. We are bombarded with programs, commercials, billboards, humor, and music that promote what's dirty, selfish, greedy, and godless. Unless you live in a monastery, you get a truckload of dirt dumped on you every day. And that's how often you need a spiritual shower—just like the guys in the locker room. A daily "Bible-bath."

A daily "Bible-bath" is a basic necessity. In each twenty-four-hour period you are confronted with the dirt and smell of life in a lost world. You need time alone in God's holy and cleansing presence, time when you and He are together exclusively. Every day let God's viewpoint wash your soul and return you to a pure starting point for the day. That way, though some dirt will accumulate on you, it shouldn't be there for long.

Remove the dirt every day. If you let the dirt of the world accumulate, it will wear you down and you will start to accept as normal and acceptable what God calls sick and repulsive. I won't let my son go a day without a shower—he's a high school athlete. I know God expects His children to take a spiritual shower every day, too. After all, in a spiritual sense, you and I really are living in a locker room. We can't avoid the odor, but we can wash it off with a daily "Bible-bath."

**T**here's an art to shopping for produce. You can't just buy the first apple or tomato you see. You must first know how to "squeeze the lettuce." My wife taught me how to do that. She also taught me how to check for holes and dents in apples and peaches. You just don't take the first one on the pile. You learn to check how yellow those bananas are, or how green, or how black. There are ways to tell if a given vegetable is one you should buy. It's much tougher to shop for a spiritual leader you can trust. But there *is* a way to tell. In a world that offers too many "bad apples," it's important to know...

# How to Shop in a Spiritual Supermarket

Each day it's getting tougher to know which spiritual leaders you can trust. You can squeeze the lettuce, you can look for the dents and the holes in the apples and peaches, but how can you recognize truly sound spiritual leaders? We live at a time when many so-called Christian heroes have let down their followers. These heroes might have said spiritual things, led spiritual causes, and given spiritual counsel—and then something happens that exposes their hypocrisy. It makes us hold back and wonder who it is we can trust.

Though the Bible makes clear that we are not supposed to have our eyes on man, God does establish leaders for His people. He does raise up teachers. There *are* authentic spiritual leaders. God wants us to be able to receive teachings and experience His love through people. Yet many of these leaders have let us down. How are we to tell whether a pastor is a leader from God or a person "doing his own thing" in God's name? One way to tell is to look to an individual in the Bible Jesus held up as a model leader, John the Baptist. Jesus said of him, "Among those born of women there has not risen anyone greater than John the Baptist" (Matthew 11:11). Can you think of a stronger endorsement than that? Jesus said that John the Baptist was a genuine spiritual leader. Out of the life of John we get a crucial test for a pastor, Christian musician, TV or radio personality, or youth leader. In John 3:30 John the Baptist asserts, speaking of Jesus: "He must become greater; I must become less." The King James Version says, "He must increase, but I must decrease." Does a spiritual leader leave you thinking more about him or more about Jesus? Where is the spotlight? On his organization, his goals, his programs? Or on Jesus? An authentic man or woman of God, like John the Baptist, puts himself in the background. The leader "doing his own thing" sprinkles his talk with *I, me, mine.* Is the "spotlight test" the only gauge of the spirituality of a leader? No. But it's a good start.

Look at your own life. Are you in a leadership position? If you are, measure yourself against the standard set by John the Baptist. Who is the spotlight? You, the leader? Or Christ the Savior? Genuinely spiritual leaders, the ones you can trust, are the ones who put Jesus in the spotlight and make you think of Him and forget the messenger. In the crowded spiritual supermarket in which we shop, that's how we know whom we can "buy."

**H**ave you been called by a computer yet? Probably so. You have to be really lonely to appreciate a call like that. Your number is computer-dialed by someone with something to sell, and you get a call something like this: "Hello, this is Bruce. I'm a computer, and I'd like to have a word with you about—" Oops—wait a minute! That's not a very meaningful communication experience. Bruce does all the talking. There's no use even trying to tell the computer caller anything. He does only one-way communication. God gets a lot of calls like that. So what's the style when *you* call...

# Monologue? Or Dialogue?

When Samuel, the great judge of Israel, was a young boy in training in the home of Eli, the priest at the Temple, he heard one night a voice calling for him. Samuel thought the voice was Eli's, so he ran to his side, calling, "Here am I" (v. 4). But the old priest had not called Samuel. A second and a third time Samuel heard the voice and ran to Eli. The third time the old priest "realized that the Lord was calling the boy" (v. 8), and he gave Samuel instructions to follow if he should hear the voice again.

Samuel did hear the voice again. "The Lord came and stood there, calling as at the other times, 'Samuel! Samuel!' Then Samuel said, 'Speak, for your servant is listening' " (v. 10). "Speak, for your servant is listening." That's the right approach. But most of us rewrite the verse. We say, "Listen, Lord, your servant is speaking," and we run into the throne room from which the universe is governed, dump what we have to say, and run out again. Sort of like Bruce the computer! Before the Lord can say what He has to say, we have left the room.

If I came to your house and sat down in the living room and talked for an hour solid, never let you say or ask anything, and then went to the door and walked out, you'd say, "Man, is that Hutchcraft guy rude!" Well, we do it to God all the time. And it *is* rude!

God says to us, "Be still and know that I am God" (Psalm 46:10); "wait on the Lord (Psalm 27:14). Elijah found God's voice was not in the wind, not in the fire, and not in the earthquake, but was "a still small voice" (1 Kings 19:12, KJV). God speaks when you give Him the space—the silence—in which to do it.

We are uncomfortable with silence. When things are silent it seems to us that nothing's happening. But with God, silence is where it happens!

Feel free to give God your thanks, your needs, your hurts, your praise, and your questions, but then allow time in your devotions for quiet. Linger in God's presence. Give Him opportunity to show you a perspective you didn't have before—to break a log-jam in your mind, to show you a solution or an insight, to say something to your heart, to give you a new way of looking at a person, to show you a step you ought to take. Those are blessed moments. Moments we busy Christians miss!

If you are like me, listening to God will take practice and self-control. But it's worth it! God has much He wants to show you, but He is unlikely to interrupt while you are talking. So let prayer be a dialogue, not a monologue. You are not a computer-caller, are you? Listen. Let God write His thoughts on the blank slate of your waiting heart. God deserves better than a one-way call.

**W**e keep finding our family in the comic strips. One of the kids will come to me, with the cartoon page from the newspaper in hand, and say, "Here we are, Dad!" And, sure enough, there we are. Often it's the comic strip "Family Circus." The man behind it obviously has children of his own. Whenever the parents find a mess or something eaten, or missing, they start asking the children what happened. Needless to say, no one ever takes responsibility. The parents always end up ruefully concluding that the culprit was "the ghost of 'not me.' "

That "not me" spirit keeps a lot of folks from being able to say, "It's my fault." Maybe it's time we had a ...

## Funeral for a Ghost

David the king knew how to bury the ghost of "not me." You know the story. David, in the middle of a glorious, serving time in his life, committed with Bathsheba the ugly sin of adultery. When the prophet Nathan confronted David with his sin, he could have offered excuses. He could have said, "I was lonely that night. I couldn't help myself. I was vulnerable." He could have said, "Well, she was tempting, and she was willing. She could have said no." David could have said, "Well, I was under a lot of stress as king. You know, it's hard being the king of Israel." But that is not what he said. He took responsibility for his sin. "Wash away all my iniquity and cleanse me from my sin," he prayed, "for I know my transgressions, and my sin is always before me. Against you, you only, have I sinned and done what is evil in your sight" (Psalm 51:2-4). He knew who was responsible. "Cleanse me with hyssop, and I will be clean; wash me, and I will be whiter than snow" (v. 7). What a contrast that is with the attitude too often exhibited by those caught in adulterous activity. Claims of being manipulated and victimized are brought forth in an effort to justify sin. But that was not David's way. "I know my transgressions," he acknowledged, "and my sin is ever before me."

Where do we stand when it comes to acknowledging our guilt? Are we quick to rationalize our sin—to blame our upbringing, our parents, our friends, our school, our office, the atmosphere around us, our environment, the enormity of the temptation? God asks, "Who is to blame for what you are doing?" You say, "Not me!" And there's the ghost of "not me"! Blame-shifting began in the Garden of Eden with Adam and Eve. "It's *her* fault," "No, it's *his* fault," "No, it's the *serpent's* fault." There is no healing, no forgiveness, and no peace until you join David in saying, "I am without excuse, Lord. It's sin—I call it what you call it. And I accept full responsibility for it. I quit blaming anything or anyone around me. I'm dirty, Lord. I need to be clean again by the blood of Christ."

Maybe you've been dodging your responsibility for what you have done. In doing so, you are only compounding the damage for that sin. Confession contains the damage. That ghost of "not me" will keep you from the peace you need. "It *is* me, Lord." Let's have a funeral for that ghost!

**T**here's nothing quite as boring as hearing a repetition of information you've heard before. I fly quite a lot, so I hear the flight attendant's announcement many, many times. To be honest, I don't pay a lot of attention to it because it is so predictable! Usually. The other day was an exception. We had a flight attendant who kept throwing in humorous surprises and fresh ways of saying things. He had our attention. Everybody listened to him! "We're preparing for landing," he said, "and you need to put your seats in the upright, most uncomfortable position." We all laughed! Then he said, "The captain has turned on the seatbelt sign, which is an indication he has finally found the airport." I loved it! It was unpredictable! That attendant knew something about communication: if you have important information to communicate, don't be predictable! Find a way to make important announcements into...

## *Interesting Announcements*

God gave mothers and fathers important announcements to make to their children. He talks about those announcements in Deuteronomy 6. "Love the Lord your God with all your heart and with all your soul and with all your strength. These commandments that I give you today are to be upon your hearts. Impress them on your children" (vv. 6-7a). We try to do that in our household. If you're a Christian parent, I'm sure you, also, try to impress the ways of God, the teachings of God, and the boundaries of God on your children.

Sometimes our children respond to our efforts with the same

disinterest I have for predictable airline announcements. "Here we go again," they say. They know what we are going to say before we have said it. It isn't enough that we go through the motions of teaching our children about the Lord. We need to teach them in ways and in places that are not predictable. We need to find means of getting their attention.

Moses showed the way. "Talk about them when you sit at home and when you walk along the road, when you lie down and when you get up" he said (v. 7). If Bible truths are always presented in the same old way and in the same old places, the listeners will soon be immune to the message. We have practiced responses to a sermon, to family devotions, to Christian meetings. We know what to expect and how to act. It's all so predictable. But there's something disarming about God-talk in the middle of everyday activity—the classroom of everyday life! When we're walking with our children, when we're riding in the car with them, when we're tucking them into bed at night, we can present Bible truths in a fresh way. The best place for your son to see God at work may be at a baseball field! Maybe on the way to the store with you, your grandchild will raise a question that provides a teachable moment. Debriefing your daughter about her day over a Big Mac or in those mellow bedtime moments as you tuck her into bed. Riding, walking, exercising, having a special date with you—these are the classrooms of everyday life. Don't depend on formal settings to do the job of introducing God to your child. Your children may tune out those formal announcements. Look for God together, in the ordinary, relaxed, casual, everyday things. As a parent, you have the blessed responsibility of passing on God's announcements to the children He has entrusted to you. Make sure those announcements aren't just true, but are interesting too.

**W**hen I was in high school, I was part of a very active Youth For Christ Bible quiz program. I still remember a good deal of what I learned studying the Bible in that highly competitive atmosphere. Excitement was high when a competition began. Believe it or not, sometimes thousands of people were in the audience. Champion quiz teams pitted against one another were seated on chairs equipped to register precisely who got off his chair first. That person would have first opportunity to answer the question. Now, if he jumped up while the question was being asked—the best way to make sure he got the opportunity to answer—he had to finish the question correctly and then give the answer. So the quizmaster instructed the participants to "Jump as soon as you think you can finish the question." Many times we competitors were strung so tight we jumped too soon—ridiculously too soon! For example, we would be quizzing on the whole gospel of John, and the quizmaster would say, "Wha—" and suddenly you'd see three people on their feet! He'd call, "Number one." And "number one" almost always lost the question! "Wha—!" Who could figure that out? No one could. You would always lose when you jumped too soon.

I guess we all lose sometimes because of...

# *Jumping Before You've Heard It All*

Proverbs 18:13 reminds me of those Bible quizzes. "He who answers before listening—that is his folly and his shame." There is a

New Testament version of that proverb: James 1:19 says, "Everyone should be quick to listen, slow to speak, and slow to become angry." We've rewritten that one, haven't we? We are quick to speak and slow to listen. But notice the sequence the Bible prescribes. The listening comes before the speaking. Solomon tells us that we ought to be ashamed of ourselves, that it is our folly and our shame to speak before we listen. But we rush on heedlessly. We hear the beginning of what someone is trying to tell us, and we assume we know the rest. Like the Bible quizzers, we jump up with our reply. It happens in our marriage conversations, in conversations between parents, and conversation among parents and children. We anticipate what we think will be said and then don't understand one another.

Biblically wise people don't just listen to the sentence, they listen to the whole paragraph! They don't respond to the opening line, they listen to the whole page. When you jump too soon, you usually end up misunderstanding what's being said. You react to the symptom, not the problem. The person you are with doesn't pay attention to what you are saying because you didn't pay attention to him. Conflict erupts. Walls go up.

If you played a tape of what you said today, would you hear yourself being "quick to speak"? If so, you may be inflicting hurt, creating frustration, engendering misunderstanding, and causing people to tune you out. They won't want to talk with you anymore. When it comes to listening how are you perceived by your mate? Your children? Your parents? Your friends? Maybe some of those persons have stopped trying to communicate with you. Tell them you want another chance. It will take patience and self-control to listen not just to a person's words but to his heart. But it is worth it, for according to the Word of God, it is foolish not to listen before you speak. And, of course, part of the fruit of the Spirit is patience and self-control (Galatians 5). That's what it takes to listen before you speak. "Dear Lord, give me patience and self-control. Teach me, Lord, to listen." Take it from an old Bible quizzer who sometimes couldn't wait. When you jump too soon, you usually get it wrong!

I t is always thrilling to return to my office after I've been away for a few days. My desk is covered with call-slips! Sometimes I tell my secretary she might as well paper the walls with them—there are enough! Many of the call slips have to do with invitations to speak, and I enjoy that. The problem is that sometimes it seems as though everybody wants to do something on the same weekend. A winter retreat on Washington's Birthday weekend, a Friday night dinner in the spring, camps and conferences in July and August. You run out of weeks in a hurry. Well, there *is* a way to relieve the pressure that accumulates on a particular week or weekend—*decide*. Just decide which invitation you are going to accept. Once you make a commitment, it's easy to handle any future requests. But as long as you are undecided, things are up for grabs. Maybe that's why you're feeling so much pressure lately.

The demands on you cry out for an answer to the question...

# How Do You Spell Relief?

Daniel 1:8 has to do with commitments. Let me give you a little background just in case you slept during Sunday school when they were covering the life of Daniel. Daniel had been carried away from his homeland of Israel, and he was now in the Babylonian Empire, one of a select group of young men who were being groomed for leadership. The Babylonians wanted the young men to follow a special diet to ensure that they became strong and wise and able to exercise the most effective leadership in the kingdom. Unfortunately, the diet the Babylonians proposed would cause Daniel to defile himself according to Jewish law. Daniel 1:8 records Daniel's choice: "But Daniel resolved not to defile himself with the royal food and wine, and he asked the chief official for permission not to defile himself this way. Now God had caused the official to show favor and sympathy to Daniel." The rest of the story tells us that when Daniel had stated his convictions he was allowed the chance to substitute a diet acceptable under Jewish law. At the end of the trial period, it was evident that Daniel and the Hebrew young men with him, who were also on the special diet, were much healthier than the young men who had eaten Babylonian fare. Daniel had a meteoric rise to power in the Babylonian kingdom.

Daniel was under heavy pressure to do something he didn't believe in. You may be under the same type of pressure. You're in an environment where wrong is considered normal. There is pressure to acquire sexual experience, and mockery for you if you don't. There is pressure to lie for the company, or to cheat in school, or to laugh at what's dirty. Perhaps there is pressure to party. Or perhaps the elite in your circle have a habit of putting people down, or of gossiping and back-stabbing. Heavy pressure! I believe Daniel's answer to peer pressure should be yours. Make up your mind, settle the matter, take your stand. Daniel let people know what to expect from him, and they backed off! It may be that you haven't taken your stand, so those in your circle keep coming back to you because they're not sure what to expect. But if you clearly told them your convictions and consistently stood by those convictions they *would* know what to expect from you. They might not agree with your convictions, but they will back off once you take your stand—and probably respect you for it. In many cases, they may even wish they had similar courage.

How do you spell relief from peer pressure? C-O-N-V-I-C-T-I-O-N. CONVICTION! As long as the people around you think you are like them, or that you are undecided, they will push you again and again. Once you tell them to expect you to be different, they will let you be different. Have you had enough peer pressure? Try some relief.

Decide where your line is. Let people know. And never cross that line. The pressure is because you haven't clearly decided. The relief comes from CONVICTION.

**I**t had to be one of the most insecure afternoons of my life. Our committee had been meeting at a hotel for two days straight. Finally, our chairman, a severe taskmaster, said, "All right, guys, how about a couple of hours in the pool here?" We said, "All right, the pool, the suana—we deserve a break today!" There was only one problem. He had told most of the fellows before the meeting that we might be swimming but somehow neglected to tell my best friend and me. We had come totally unprepared. We had no swimwear whatsoever. But we really didn't want to pass up the pool and the sauna. So I went down to the gift shop and asked, "Do you have any swim trunks for sale?" The lady said, "Well, yes, I have some paper trunks."

"What?!"

"Yes," she said. "They're reinforced paper trunks. They're only two dollars."

Well, they were my only choice. So I bought them. But it was an insecure afternoon for my friend and me as we sat in the sauna in those paper trunks. "I'm happy to report there was no modesty crisis that day, but I didn't keep the trunks. I used them and threw them away.

That experience impressed on me the difference between what we know we are going to wear for only a little while and what you know we are going to be wearing for a long time. Paper trunks are worth maybe $2.00, surely not much more, and they are thrown away as soon as they have been worn once. But there is a wardrobe that is permanent. It's important to understand the difference between...

# Paper Trunks and a Permanent Wardrobe

There are many things on which you can base your identity. Most of those roles are "paper trunks" you wear for a little while and then throw away. There *is* an identity, however, that you will always have if you have committed your life to Jesus Christ. Paul talks about that identity in Ephesians 1. Notice the two words that are repeated four times in the passage. "In him we were also chosen, having been predestined according to the plan of him who works out everything in conformity with the purpose of His will, in order that we, who were the first to hope in Christ, might be for the praise of his glory. And you also were included in Christ when you heard the word of truth, the gospel of your salvation. Having believed, you were marked in Christ with a seal, the promised Holy Spirit" (vv. 11-13). Where is your identity? It is "in Christ." You may have many "identities" in your life. In high school you may have asked, "Is there life after high school?" You lived as though life *was* high school, and you made all your choices on the basis of that assumption. College was another "life." I know professional football players who say, "Is there life after football?"

Is there life after whatever company or organizaton you work for? After retirement? After you lose your mate or your parents? Life is a series of new starts. What happens after the children are gone? Kindergarten, college, marriage, the empty nest, job changes, retirement—all are new starts. We wear those new identities for a period of time. But if we are to find personal security, we need a transcendent identity—an identity that will be with us forever.

Paul told us what that identity is. It is to be "in Christ." A believer will always belong to Jesus Christ—after high school, when college is a memory, when he is still single, when he is married, when he has been widowed, when he is raising his kids, when his kids have left home, when he dies. We tend to pay a very high price for our temporary identities, our "paper trunks," far higher that we should. We will rarely see most of our high school friends after we graduate. Yet in high school we compromise to hide our eternal relationship with Christ because we're scared. How sad to play by the rules of the crowd just to be accepted at school, in the dorm, or on the job. How sad to sacrifice our loyalty to Christ for something that is only transitory. Believers belong to Christ forever! Why not really be what you'll always be? Don't waste your treasure on the "paper trunks" of life. Put your treasure in the permanent wardrobe that will never wear out.

**I** was a "Flash Gordon" freak when I was a kid. Now, in case you've led a deprived life and are wondering *Flash who?*, let me bring you up to date. Flash Gordon was that intergalactic hero made famous in a serialized movie filmed in the 1930s. No, I did not see the movie when it first came out, but the studio issued movie after movie in the series, so eventually I did see it. Today episodes are sometimes shown on late night TV. Every episode ended with Flash in a jam. He was always just about to be destroyed by a space monster or a death ray—and you were sure there was no way he could extricate himself. But he always did. There is always a way out for you, too, if you are working for the right director. He specializes in...

## Flash Gordon Rescues

You probably have had a life full of close calls, just like old Flash Gordon, except his were in the movies and yours were for real. The same goes for me. There's another man whose life was full of close calls—the apostle Paul. He talks about those calls in 2 Timothy 3:10-11: "You [know the] persecutions, sufferings—what kinds of things happened to me at Antioch, Iconium and Lystra, the persecutions I endured. Yet the Lord rescued me from all of them." Now, when I reread those verses the other day, I thought of Flash Gordon. Flash Gordon was always rescued from the close calls he experienced. That's the bottom line for the child of God. God will sometimes let us go to the edge, but He will never let us go over. "The Lord rescued me out of them all," Paul said. You and I can say that. Look at the past episodes in your life.

The time the money ran out, or the time when your friends or your family ran out, or when your strength ran out. Maybe you've been so lonely at times that you thought you couldn't stand it another day. Maybe you've been frustrated because every door seemed to slam shut in your face. There were things and people you had depended on—remember? And they were suddenly gone. Or maybe you were hopelessly buried in work, responsibilities, and stress, and you said, "I'll never get out of this mess!" You've been to the edge of desperation. But remember? The Lord rescued you out of them all.

Maybe you are again in a perilous or painful place. This time it looks as though "there's no way out, Flash." But then it's looked like that before—and you're still here. Get some perspective, stand back, remember a lifetime of the Lord's rescues. First Corinthinans 10:13 says, "God...will not let you be tempted beyond what you can bear, [but] will always provide a way out so that you can stand up under it." He will let you bear heavy loads but never more than you can handle. Jesus is your Savior. He has already accomplished the toughest rescue of all—rescue from the clutches of sin! He'll change the situation, or He'll enlarge you so that you can deal with it. He *will* rescue you!

**W**hen I'm out of town I've developed the habit of turning on the television while I'm settling into a new hotel room. I like to get the local flavor, especially the weather and local news. I probably watch more television on the road than I do at home, when I almost never watch it. It's helpful to turn on the TV like that when you are traveling in the United States, but it's frustrating to do so in another country. Some time ago I was in Amsterdam for a major conference. I turned on the television while I was unpacking in my hotel room, and I saw a man earnestly communicating everything I needed to know—the local news and weather forecast—and I couldn't understand a word he was saying! It was all in Dutch! It was very frustrating. The announcer knew the information I needed, and I wanted to know it, but the information was not being conveyed in a language I could understand. You may know some folks who feel the same way about you. They're trying to tell you...

## Say It in My Language

In Acts 2 Luke describes a communications miracle that took place at the feast of Pentecost not long after Jesus' ascension. As the disciples were praying in an upper room the Holy Spirit suddenly came to indwell them. The disciples burst out into the street, preaching and praising God. And they were understood by the people there—even though the people came from many parts of the world and the disciples had never been given linguistic training. "All of them [the disciples who were gathered together for prayer in the upper room] were filled with the Holy Spirit and began to speak

58

in other tongues as the Spirit enabled them. Now there were staying in Jerusalem God-fearing Jews from every nation under heaven. When they heard this sound, a crowd came together in bewilderment, because each one heard them speaking in his own language" (vv. 5-6). The people listening to the disciples said, "We hear them declaring the wonders of God in our own tongues" (v. 11*b*). That was the key—they were hearing the good news in their own language.

Now, in one sense, the event that took place on the Pentcost after Christ's resurrection was a miracle for a special occasion. But it is still true that our message has no effect until a person hears it in a "language" he can understand. There are people around us all the time with whom we are trying to communicate the gospel, but we are like the Dutch newsman I heard. He was presenting the information but not in a language I could understand.

We Christians have a similar language problem. When we became Christians we started to pick up a "Christian" vocabulary. We got used to expressing Christ in "religious" terms. But they're terms that a lost person doesn't understand! There may be someone close to you who is rejecting Christ. Maybe he is rejecting Him because he has never heard about Him in his own "heart" language. Unbelievers don't understand our church talk. They need to hear the gospel expressed in the language of sports, or business, or music, or gardening, or parenting, or computers, or medicine. It has got to be something they can relate to. It's lazy to present the message in your own comfortable religious jargon. Think about that lost person, walk a mile in his shoes, learn his vocabulary. Look at his interests, and discover how the truths of the gospel can be communicated and illustrated in those terms. I sat in the Dutch hotel room and murmured, "Say it in my language, will you?" Well, there's someone near you, someone without Christ, someone waiting for words he can understand. Say it in his language!

**T**hree New York City boys broke into a zoo. One of them climbed into the polar bear area to swim in the moat surrounding it. You saw the result on the news. The boy was attacked by the bears and brutally killed. I was fascinated by an interview given not long afterward by the park commissioner of New York City. "You know," he said, "bears are protrayed to children as friendly, even cuddly animals but in reality they are carnivorous killers." He was right. We've got Winnie the Pooh, Paddington Bear, Smokey the Bear, and Snuggles. The image is cuddly. But the reality is deadly. And not just in bear country. We are surrounded by...

## Cuddly Killers

James 1:15 is a revealing verse. "After desire has conceived, it gives birth to sin; and sin, when it is full-grown, gives birth to death." It's interesting—a sequence scenario that ends in the death of a relationship, or of self-respect, or of a reputation, that may even end in physical death, starts out only as a desire, an enticement. Sin looks inviting sometimes. It looks like so much fun—maybe like those polar bears. But it is a killer! For in reality there is nothing more beautiful than good and nothing more ugly than evil.

Our imaginations tell us just the opposite. We imagine that there's nothing more ugly than truth and nothing more beautiful than evil. So we flirt with that from which we should flee. Maybe you are playing in the bear cage of sin. The wrong still looks cuddly and exciting. You're in a relationship you never should have gotten into. Perhaps you're doing things in a relationship that seem good right now though you know the Bible condemns them. Maybe you've fallen for the pressure to try some things that are wrong. Maybe you are mentally playing with sin right now—fantasizing, picturing, considering. You're doing something you never thought you would do as God's child. Maybe you're thinking about something you know is wrong and which you think you'll never do. The thought is still just a desire. And what happens? Desire becomes sin. You think, you put your thoughts into action, and then you pay. The relationship that seemed so good now destroys you. The things you knew were wrong but did anyway now result in your harm. The compromise that promised love, or attention, or excitement now leads to dying.

A New York boy underestimated the danger of a bear, and he died as a result. You may be underestimating the danger of a "desirable" sin. If you don't get out now, while you still can, it will turn on you and kill everything you care about! No matter how warm and cuddly sin may appear, it is a killer. Don't play with a killer!

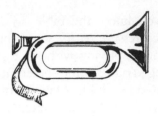

**A** few years ago our local high school football team made the most dramatic turnaround I think I've ever seen in a high school team. The season before they scored in only two games. Then a new coach took over—and suddenly they were in the state championship, and have been in the top levels ever since. They have a coach who molds winners. I pointed out to my son one of the reasons this coach is so successful. He had told me which position he'd like to play. I said, "Listen, you need to trust that coach and let him assign your position, because one of his gifts is knowing what position each fellow will play best." I've seen players strongly resist the position the coach assigned them. "Hey, coach," they've complained, "I want to be...," they'd begin. "No," he'd say, "you're going to play *this* position." And they'd end up being all-conference and all-country—and thanking the coach. So I told my son to trust the coach for the best position to play. It's good advice for all of us to...

# Let the Coach Place You

In John 21:17c-22a Jesus talks to Peter about the ministry He is giving the apostle. Jesus tells Peter to "feed his sheep," and then He adds a sobering reflection of the future. " 'I tell you the truth, when you were younger you dressed yourself and went where you wanted; but when you are old you will stretch out your hands, and someone else will dress you and lead you where you do not want to go.' Jesus said this to indicate the kind of death by which Peter would glorify God. Then he said to him 'Follow me!'

"Peter turned and saw [John] following them....When Peter

saw him, he asked, 'Lord, what about him?'

"Jesus answered, 'If I want him to remain alive until I return what is that to you? You must follow me.' "

It's interesting. Peter seems to be questioning the coach. He's questioning the position he's going to play compared to the position John is going to play. We, too, question the coach—but we shouldn't, for the Lord has a position on His team that you were created to play, gifted to play. The Lord is saying to you, as He did to Peter, "Don't worry about somebody else's position; you play your assignment."

First Corinthians 12:6 tells us that "there are different kinds of working, but the same God works all of them in all men." That includes all believers. The manifestation of the Spirit is given to each one for the common good. You have to believe that God has a position for you to play—in His family, in His work on earth—because the Bible says all believers have a position. You need to trust the Lord to give you the assignment where you can do the most. It may not be the position you wanted to play. Maybe you wanted to be in front, and He has you working backstage. Maybe you wanted to be working backstage, and He has you working in front. Maybe you wanted to lead, and He has you being a follower. Or maybe you want to follow, and He's pushing you to be a leader. Maybe He's teaching you to do humble tasks. Maybe you want to be *doing*, and He's assigned you to be *preparing*. Our coach not only sees our talent and potential, He created it! Don't chafe if He asks you to play a position different from the one you want. He created you for a specific assignment. He knows where you will play the best. he knows which position will do the most for you and for His kingdom. Hang in there on the assignment He has given you. There you can contribute the most, learn the most, and share the most. Let the coach place you. He knows how to produce champions.

**I**f you ever saw my oldest son eat a hamburger—and how quickly it disappears—I'm sure you would find it hard to believe that there was a time when he was too young to eat one. Yet we have the home movies to prove it. We have super-eight movies of him as a baby eating the mush that only babies eat. He didn't yet have equipment to chew a hamburger. So, we fed him the smooth, beaten-to-death version of the real thing. No chewing, no effort—it just slides down. But even though he has to work harder on meat these days, he has no desire to go back to the "old days" of baby food. That's because the best food requires some effort. A lot of people spend their lives in baby food jars because they are...

## Lazy Eaters

Hebrews 5:11-14 is about lazy eaters. "We have much to say about [Christ]," the writer asserts, "but it is hard to explain because you are slow to learn. In fact, though by this time you ought to be teachers, you need someone to teach you the elementary truths of God's Word all over again. You need milk, not solid food! Anyone who lives on milk, being still an infant, is not acquainted with the teaching about righteousness. But solid food is for the mature, who by constant use have trained themselves to distinguish good from evil." Paul is writing to Christians who had insisted on undemanding food—milk. They were lazy eaters.

That kind of laziness is all too common among North American Christians—the most entertained Christians in history. We are spoiled by radio preachers, TV shows, seminars, and Christian celebrities. We want—we expect—our sermons to be funny, exciting, and challenging. We want our speakers to be entertainers. We expect our teachers to be brief and to the point. We want our pastor to chop up our food for us and give it to us "Gerberized." We like "melt-in-your-mouth" messages that don't take a lot of effort to hear. We let gifted pastors and speakers do 80 percent of the chewing for us. All we have to do is meet them 20 percent of the way. We don't have to invest much effort in what these men have to say.

But there are speakers who require careful attention from an audience and a determination to follow along with them, a willingness to make one's own applications and connections. These people have a good deal to say from the Lord and they require that their listeners come 40, 50, 75 percent of the way. That is true of some writers, too. You may say, "Well, this is hard to read." And yet, it's worth sticking with it, it's worth chewing.

A spiritual leader doesn't have to be funny or have tons of charisma in order to feed you. He doesn't have to be a Billy Graham, or a Chuck Swindoll, or a James Dobson. God has put you under the teaching of someone who cares about you. Don't expect that leader, pastor, teacher, or writer to do all of the chewing for you. Give your God-appointed teachers your very best. When you listen to them, be prepared to chew, to work for a good meal. You're too big for baby food! Lazy eaters never grow up. Don't be too lazy to chew a good piece of meat.

When your wife is as able a photographer as mine, trips can be a very different kind of experience. You'll be riding along, and all of a sudden, she'll say, "Can you stop, honey?" I don't know why, but I stop. Turns out she sees a great picture, which I too see when she invites me to look through the telescopic lens of her camera. The lens screens out distracting surroundings and magnifies the details you would otherwise miss. It focuses on the best view of that subject. We could use such a lens on our relationships. After all...

## The Lens Improves the Picture

In John 17 Jesus is praying His great high priestly prayer before His arrest. What Jesus sees in His disciples is different from what one would conclude from an earthly perspective. In verse 6, Jesus looks at who the disciples are. At that point and from an earthly perspective they look like guys who are ready to abandon ship. In a few minutes, when the soldiers come, they will indeed do just that. But Jesus sees them differently when He's praying. He says, "I have revealed you to those you gave me out of the world. They were yours; you gave them to me and they have obeyed your word" (v. 6). He sees them in a higher way than we would. We would see the disciples as men battling over who was going to be the greatest in the kingdom of heaven and thereby compromising Jesus. We would see them as self-centered and preoccupied with saving their own skins. Yet Jesus says in verse 14, "They are not of the world anymore than I am of the world." To us, the disciples seem worldly. But Jesus sees them through a different lens. They were on the threshold of deserting Jesus, and yet, in verse 20, He talks about those who are going to believe through them. They were at war with one another, arguing over who was going to be the greatest in the kingdom of heaven, and yet, in verse 23, Jesus says they are going to be in complete unity. They look different when they are seen through the eyes of prayer.

Jesus sees Himself as well through the lens of prayer. He is about to be rejected and crucified, yet, He says in verse 5, "Glorify me in your presence with the glory I had with you before the world began." He sees the glorified person He really is.

One purpose of prayer is to make us see people as God sees them—and to see ourselves as God sees us. It is an exciting way to pray. "Lord, let me look through Your lens." Maybe the one you need to see through the lens of prayer is someone you love, or someone you're worried about, or someone who frustrates or angers you, someone who's opposing you. "Lord, what do you see when You look at that person? I want to see that." You wouldn't believe how a marriage can change if the partners consistently try to see what God sees in their mate. The same is true of the relationship you have with your parents, with your children, with your friends, with your pastor. Ask God to let you see yourself and those around you through His lens. "Show me, Father, what You see when You look at me and my life right now." Much will change when, through the lens of prayer, you screen out distracting surroundings, magnify details you would otherwise miss, and focus on the best view. God's lens improves the picture!

**A**n ordinary place can become a special place. There's a tree in Grant Park in Chicago that was Karen's and my tree when we were courting. We spent a lot of time there. To other people the tree is just another tree, but to us it's special. In the life of our family other spots have become special, places where we shared memorable experiences. You probably can say the same. Ordinary places, places that are no big deal to anyone else, are special to you because they are associated with tender moments. To someone else, that place is just another rock, another beach, another street—but to you, it glows as a place of great significance. We all have "ordinaries" that are special. I have even seen...

## Ordinary Rooms That Glow

Genesis 28 is about the life of Jacob. "Jacob left Beersheba and set out for Haran. When he had reached a certain place, he stopped for the night because the sun had set. Taking one of the stones there, he put it under his head and lay down to sleep." You may remember the rest of the story. That night the Lord appeared to Jacob dramatically through the vision of the ladder that reached up to heaven, the angels descending upon it. The Scripture tells us that "when Jacob awoke from his sleep, he thought 'Surely, the Lord is in this place, and I was not aware of it.' He was afraid and said, 'How awesome is this place. This is none other than the house of God; this is the gate of heaven.' " Jacob had been on an ordinary mission. He was just traveling, and he had come to an average spot, a "certain place." But by the end of the passage, he's calling it the house of God. Because of the presence of the Lord, an ordinary place had become a sanctified place.

I've been traveling more these last few years than I had before, and as a result, I see a good many motel rooms. As I walk into a motel room with my suitcase in hand, I'm learning to dedicate that room and all that happens in it to the Lord Jesus. When you are away from home, when you are in a new place, it's too easy to get careless and to watch something you normally wouldn't watch, to think things you wouldn't normally think. What a difference it makes to consecrate the television, the bed, the desk, the entire room to the Lord. Suddenly a motel room becomes holy ground. It becomes your "Bethel," house of God. "Surely the Lord is in this place."

The same can happen when you consecrate the road you take, the office you visit, the waiting room you occupy. As you travel the miles alone, even a car can become a sacred place. The "ordinary" place can be the place where you meet the Lord. Perhaps it's the telephone, or a desk. Maybe it's the place where you exercise or run. Think about consecrating the everyday places in you life and letting them become God's places, where you think His thoughts and carry out His ways. I love those words of Jacob—"in a certain place"—no big place. "Surely the Lord is in this place." Well, of course, the Lord "makes" the place. Crown Him Lord of the places in which you find yourself. It will make a difference. He can make even ordinary rooms glow!

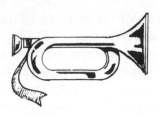

**P**robably the most traumatic event in modern American history was the assassination of John F. Kennedy. Moments from that event were captured forever in our memories. Many of us have replayed them mentally, perhaps even now, as I refer to the occasion. After the initial shock of hearing of Kennedy's death, I remember asking, "Did they get the person who did it?" I was relieved that they had a strong suspect, a man identified as Lee Harvey Oswald. *Well, good, we'll find out who and why, and justice will be done,* I thought. That wasn't to be. Jack Ruby killed Oswald as he was being moved from one police location to another—all this just two days after Kennedy's death. Oswald died, and America was deprived forever of the information he could have provided and the justice that might have resulted. All because one man interfered with the processes of justice. But then, we've all been guilty of...

# Thwarting Justice

Romans 12:17 is a radical verse. It goes against our makeup. "Do not repay evil for evil," it says. "Be careful to do what is right in the eyes of everybody." Verse 18 has a similar message. "If it is possible, as far as it depends on you, live at peace with everyone." Why? Verse 19 supplies an answer. "Do not take revenge, my friends, but leave room for God's wrath, for it is written: 'It is mine to avenge; I will repay,' says the Lord. On the contrary: 'If your enemy is hungry, feed him.' " This verse is a guarantee. It's a guarantee of justice. God will pay every bill in full. He will avenge every wrong. He will do so in just the right way and at just the right time—unless we pull a "Jack Ruby," and try to help the process along. Notice the wording. "Do not take revenge...but leave room for God's wrath." That is intriguing. When we try to punish someone who has hurt us, we interfere with God's perfect justice. We crowd Him out! We say, "God, I was the one who was hurt, and I'll take care of this, thank you." We become the avenger. We become the one who will make it right. We become the punisher.

The usual excuse for taking this role is "I just want justice." Is that really so? Do we want justice? Or do we want satisfaction? If it's justice we really want, we should leave it to God and keep our hands out of it! There is a guarantee in the Bible of the justice of God. In Genesis 18:25 Abraham calls God "the judge of all the earth": "Will not the Judge of all the earth do right?" God will not let a person get away with his sin. He may be delaying that judgment. He may let a person play out his string until the inevitable kick-back comes and the law of "sowing and reaping" takes place. Leave room for God's justice. Your responsibility is to love the person who wronged you, to feed your enemy if he's hungry, and to seek peace. The judge of all the earth will take care of your situation. Leave it with Him. Don't stop the process of God's justice with the bullet of your revenge!

**I**f you're in law enforcement, fingerprints are your friend. If you're a photographer or a baseball card collector—and I have one of each at my house—fingerprints are not your friend. My wife, the photographer, tells me that fingerprints ruin slides. You might be able to find out "who did it" by the fingerprint, but that won't mend the damage to the slide. And she's got some that are pretty valuable. My son, the baseball card collector, tells me that fingerprints can ruin cards and take them out of mint condition, where they're most valuable. If you handle the cards too much, you will ruin them. That's the way it is with many things in life—things such as...

## *Fingerprints on Your Future*

Genesis 27 tells of an incident in the life of Rebekah, Isaac's wife. When her twin sons, Jacob and Esau, were still in the womb she had received a promise that the older son, Esau, would serve the younger, Jacob: "Two nations are in your womb, and two peoples from within you will be separated; one people will be stronger than the other, and the older will serve the younger" (Genesis 25:23). Jacob would receive the blessing that would give him the dominant position. But for some time it looked as though that wasn't going to happen. Now, in Genesis 27, it seemed as though Isaac was near death (though he would live for many more years), and yet he had not proclaimed the blessing for his sons.

On the day recorded in Genesis 27 Isaac asked Esau to go and out into the fields, hunt his favorite game, and bring back meat that could be made into a savory meal. Then Isaac would give Esau the blessing. It looked as if Jacob wasn't going to get the blessing after all. Enter Rebekah. The stage mother would save the day. She hurried to Jacob and said, " 'My son, let the curse fall on me. Just do what I say; go and get [the game] for me.'

"So he went and got them and brought them to his mother, and she prepared some tasty food, just the way his father liked it. Then Rebekah took the best clothes of Esau her older son, which she had in the house, and put them on her younger son Jacob. She also covered his hands and the smooth part of his neck with the goatskins." Well, it fooled Isaac. He gave the blessing to Jacob.

Then Esau came back. He was furious and wanted to kill Jacob (v. 41). To protect Jacob's life, Rebekah sent Jacob away for what she thought would be a short exile, though it turned out to be twenty years of estrangement, twenty years with his life on hold and a family ripped apart. Rebekah was working for a good outcome, but she didn't leave the process to God. She got her fingerprints all over the future and made a mess!

Don't you make the same mistake. It may be tempting to try to help God out, to speed things up, to make happen what we think should happen, but when we do, we inevitably create a mess. One thing you will want to be sure of—that God did it, not you. When the dark times come, that assurance is all that will get you through—the assurance that you know it is God's will. "I did not manipulate this. I didn't touch it. This is God's doing."

Rebekah could have had a wonderful outcome *and* a wonderful process, but she couldn't wait for God to do it His way. Let God *give* you what you desire; don't try to *take* it. Your interference will only complicate and delay the process of God. Rebekah and Jacob learned the hard way. Don't get your fingerprints on your future!

**M**otivation—the art of getting a person to do something. We are all in the motivating business. You may be motivating people to go somewhere, to do a job, to correct a weakness in their life, to change their ways, to finish what they start, to do what you want them to do. Motivation comes in many forms. You can inspire people to do it. You can threaten them with punishment if they don't do it. You can love them into doing it. You can help them to do it, pitching in and showing them how, willing always to do your part. But the number one selection on the motivation hit parade is that tried and true method, nagging. Just keep bringing it up. Keep pushing for it. Keep talking about it. Eventually, you'll wear them down, and they'll do it just to get you off their back. Yes, nagging will get the job done. But it won't do much to enhance your relationship, for there is a down side to nagging.

It's possible that you are on the verge of that terminal condition called...

# Nagged to Death

I guess I'd have to define nagging as motivation by erosion. Just wear them down! That's what Delilah did to Samson. You remember the story. The Philistines had not been able to defeat the supernatural strength of Samson. The secret of his success lay in his hair, which the Lord had commanded never to be cut. Samson had never told anyone that. The Philistines paid beautiful Delilah to fall in love with Samson and find the secret of his strength. Three times she asked, in a cozy, romantic situation, and three times he gave her a misleading answer that proved that the Philistines could not conquer him. He had not given his secret. But, finally, he told her. The result was his capture and humiliation by the Philistines and, ultimately, his and their deaths. How did Delilah do it? Judges 16:16-17 tells us: "With such nagging she prodded him day after day, until he was tired to death. So he told her everything." Samson was worn down. He ended up doing something he was sure he would never do.

Do you know that might be happening to you right now? Maybe there are "Delilahs" in your life who want you to live as they do, to lower your standards, to compromise what you believe. They are after you day after day to do it, and you have been sure you never would, but you're weakening, aren't you? You're about to be nagged to death. Don't let it happen. Don't cave in. You think you've got pressure now? Wait until you give in to sin and compromise. You ain't seen nothin' yet.

How can you combat this nagging? Maybe you need to get away from the people who are wearing you down. Perhaps that's not possible. Then seek the Lord for daily strength to be His man or woman. This is a day by day battle. Determine to be the one who brings about change, not the one who changes. Represent Christ to the Delilahs in your life. Each morning anchor yourself to Jesus' expectations for your life and to His lordship. Keep in mind that it is not the number of times a thing is presented that makes it true. A lie repeated a thousand times is still a lie. Samson let himself be nagged to death. Don't let it happen to you.

**A** few weeks ago I had one of those "exciting" nights at Chicago's O'Hare airport. Just as our plane was getting ready to leave the gate, we were informed that the radar in the tower had suddenly gone down. Do you know what that meant? That meant that the flight controllers had no way to guide planes in or out of the airport. So they shut O'Hare down to one runway and limited traffic to visual landings. Needless to say, many of us did not go anywhere that night.

I was frustrated because I couldn't get out of the airport. Then I thought about the people up above me who couldn't land. I went outside and saw the lights of planes circling the airport in holding patterns. Many of those flights had to be diverted to other destinations. You can imagine how frustrated the passengers were. They were almost home, were in sight of Chicago, but they were not on the ground! They were almost—but not completely—in. It can be risky, this business of...

## Circling the Airport

Mark 12:28-34 tells about a man who was almost home. "One of the teachers of the law came and heard them debating. Noticing that Jesus had given them a good answer, he asked of him, 'Of all the commandments, which is the most important?' "

"The most important one," answered Jesus, "is this: 'Hear, O Israel, the Lord our God, the Lord is one. Love the Lord your God with all your heart and with all your soul and with all your mind and with all your strength.' The second is this: 'Love your neighbor as yourself.' "

The teacher replied, "You were right in saying that God is one and there is no other but him." The man went on to say that he understood that knowing God was much more than knowing about religion—it was a relationship. The man was right on target. Then Jesus spoke words that must have been sobering to a man who had all the right information but not the right application of it. He said, "You are not far from the kingdom of God." Not far, but not in. Just like those people in planes circling O'Hare field. They were in sight of the airport, in sight of home, but they had not landed.

An Air Florida flight a couple of years ago almost—but not completely—cleared a bridge as it was taking off from Washington, D.C. The plane crashed into the Potomac River, with the loss of several lives. They almost made it. Almost may describe where Jesus sees you in relation to knowing Him. You are not far from Him, but you are not in. The danger is that you may think that "close is good enough." It isn't. You could end up eighteen inches from heaven—the distance from your head to your heart. You know the facts, you respect Jesus, you even love Him, perhaps. You know how to fit into the Christian world—but it's all in your head. It's not in your heart. You've never really committed yourself to Jesus Christ. He knows it, and you know it.

God sees you circling the airport, putting off landing. Don't play with the possibility of crashing, forever, because you circled but never landed. Seek the Lord while He may be found. You are almost home. He's within sight. But you have to *land*, to consciously give the rest of your life to Jesus Christ, the one who bought you with His life. You're not far, but you're not in! Come home—today!

**B**oth of my sons own a watch. But most of the time you would never know it if you looked at their wrists. You see, they each own a watch but seldom wear it. Maybe that's typical of teenage boys. I guess kids are oblivious of time. If they *must* think about it, they usually just ask someone what time it is. If you're a parent, they usually ask you. Now, I own a watch, and I'm never without it. If I forget for a day, I'm totally lost. Now, I know that someday soon my boys will be men, with men's responsibilities, and they will have to care what time it is! It goes with maturity. Good decisions come from...

## *Knowing What Time It Is*

A famous portion of Ecclesiastes 3 observes that "there is a time for everything, and a season for every activity under heaven:...a time to plant and a time to uproot,...a time to tear down and a time to build,... a time to keep and a time to throw away, a time to tear and a time to mend" (vv. 1, 2*b*, 3*b*, 6*b*, 7*a*). God is pointing out something we are aware of just by looking at nature—that He operates in seasons. Whatever his age, a grownup child of God cares about what time it is on God's clock and operates accordingly. In fact, he is only asking for frustration if he tries to work against the time God says it is, against God's "season." There's a time when God wants you to build, and to plant, and to keep. There are other times when He wants you to tear down, to uproot, to throw away. I believe there are three seasons in God's plan for you, your family, your church, and the organizations to which you belong: the time to cut back, the time to grow, and the time to stand still.

It's one of those three times right now for you. In John 15:2, Jesus said, "He cuts off every branch in me that bears no fruit, while every branch that does bear fruit he prunes so it will be more fruitful." That's the time to cut back. Those are hard times, but they are designed to make you produce more that ever before. It may be that God is cutting you back now, not so that He can hurt you, but so that ultimately you can thrive.

Sometimes it's the time to stand still, to consolidate, to deepen relationships, to gather strength.

Frustration and failure come when we try to remove the hands on God's clock. Maybe He is cutting back right now, but you're trying to push ahead. Maybe He wants you to stand still, and you insist on growing. Maybe He's saying, "Go for it!" and you're saying, "Well, it's cozy where I am." Personal peace is a by-product of cooperating with God's timing. You'll know what season it is by His Word, by circumstances, by prayer, and by counsel. Live in His seasons! Cut when He says, "Cut." Stand still when He says, "Stand still." Grow when He says, "Grow."

You'll make "no regrets" choices if you know what time it is—on God's clock.

" **K** iller." That's the name of a game, believe it or not. In fact, it's a game that our local Youth For Christ staff teaches to teenagers. You say, "Oh, terrific! You're teaching them 'killer'?" Well, hold on just a second. When you know the rules, you may not disapprove. We teach the kids the game at conferences we hold at the Jersey shore. The rules go like this. A few people are designed in advance "killers." They can "kill" you by coming up to you and marking you with a marker they carry. But here's the catch: they can mark you only when you're alone. If they find you alone at any time during the conference, they will come up to you very quietly and put that mark on you—and you are dead! Out. The object of the game is to be the last survivor. The game generates tremendous encouragement for kids to meet other kids—not to make the mistake of being alone very often, not to go anywhere by themselves. It contributes to togetherness, believe it or not. Now, in a sense, there's a game of "Killer" going on all the time. And it's for keeps. Your survival could depend on knowing the secret of...

# Staying Alive in a Game of "Killer"

First Peter 4:8-10 says, "Above all, love each other deeply, because love covers over a multitude of sins. Offer hospitality to one another without grumbling. Each one should use whatever gift he has received to serve others, faithfully administering God's grace in its various forms." Those are great verses. They issue a call to us to stay close to each other and to serve each other. A chapter later Peter gives a good reason for our staying close to one another: "Be self-controlled and alert. Your enemy the devil prowls around like a roaring lion looking for someone to devour" (1 Peter 5:8). In other words, there's a killer on the loose, and this killer plays for keeps! He looks for people who have allowed themselves to be cut off from the group, to be alone. He preys on those who are isolated—just as in the game of "Killer."

I'm told that the African gazelle is one of the lion's favorite luncheons, but the lion will seldom attack a gazelle when he is in a herd. Instead he tries to find a gazelle that is along the edges of the herd or is grazing by himself. He'll run him down and make a lion lunch out of him. Jesus said to Peter, "Satan has asked to sift you as wheat" (Luke 22:31). That's true of you, too! You may be playing right into his hands by drifting away from the herd, away from people you need to be close to.

Imagine a circle. It might be your family, your marriage, your church, or the believers you've been close to. At one point, you were in the middle, drawing affection and support from them. But now you're hurt, or disappointed, or in conflict, and you have drifted out of that circle you need, or you're near the edge. You're spending a lot of time alone, keeping things bottled up. You are further from people, and further from God. Do you see what's happening? You've become a "Lone Ranger Christian." The devil has poisoned your close relationships so that he can isolate you for the kill. Don't let it happen! Go back! Build those bridges! Tear down those walls! Even swallow your pride if necessary. Get back to people you can pray with and share with, because you are not built to go it alone. The devil knows that. His deadly game of "Killer" will go on, but as long as you stay close to the people God gave you, you will never be where he can get you!

81

"Should I call her, Dad?" That's my teenage son. Like all boys his age, he is unsure of the response he'll get from a girl. So he asks, "Should I call her?"

It seems like yesterday that I was asking that same question. I was a teenage boy and capable of staring at the telephone for forty-five minutes, wondering if I dared call. But there were a couple of girls I didn't worry about calling. I just picked up the phone and called. It's the same with my son. In friendship, in romance, in marriage, it's a special girl who knows how to bring out the best in a fellow by...

## Making a Man Feel Safe

Proverbs 31:10-31 contains probably the greatest description in all the Bible of what a woman can be at her most womanly. She is of "noble character" and "is worth far more than rubies" (v. 1). "Her children arise and call her blessed" (v. 28a). "Her husband is respected at the city gate, where he takes his seat among the leaders of the land" (v. 23). What a tremendous description. Any woman would like to be worth more than rubies, to have her children call her blessed, and to be of noble character. Well, one of the secrets of the Proverbs 31 lady and the secret of a woman who has healthy relationships with men, who brings out the best in the men in her life, is summed up in verse 11: "Her husband has full confidence in her, and lacks nothing of value." In modern language, "Her man feels safe with her." In our world men are usually evaluated on the basis of performance—their athletic prowess, their macho image, their capacity for being under control, their success in a career. Most men will carry this performance kind of love into their relationships with women until a loving, affirming woman lets them know that they do not have to perform for her. The man she loves does not have to impress her. He is safe with her. He can share his secrets and know they will never be violated. He can be weak around her, or frustrated, or scared.

Every man needs a woman who will love the "little boy" inside him. A man may be self-assured outside but self-conscious inside. He doesn't need a woman who's a critic, or a nag, or a predator, or a competitor. Men are lonely people, for most of their relationships are superficial ones, but God raises up a special kind of woman who is able to provide a harbor for others. The Proverbs 31 lady is a mother who makes her son feel safe, a wife who makes her husband feel safe, a teacher who makes the boy in her class feel secure. The woman does not hunt men, or chase men, or use men. She wants to minister acceptance and security to the men in her world. She is, according to Proverbs 31, "a woman who fears the Lord" (v. 30*b*). She has brought her needs to the Lord. She feels safe, so she can gently and consistently provide the secure harbor a man so desperately needs. That kind of woman a man can call on anytime. She will bring out his best!

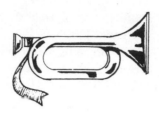

**P**eople become like the environment that surrounds them. At least that's what I've heard. If you work at IBM, you become amazingly well-organized. If you live in a college town, or work around a college, it's amazing how your vocabulary changes, even increases. Your clothing becomes perhaps a little bit more collegiate. People who live near the ocean, or in resort areas, tend to dress more casually all year long—fewer ties per square inch, so to speak. If you move from the North to the South, you may well find your pace slowing to match the environment. Conversely, I know my driving changed when I moved to the New York area. In New York, they say, there are two kinds of people—the quick and the dead. I decided to become the former. I have become a survivalist in my driving.

You may have become more like your environment than you realize. Your only defense is...

## Drawing the Line

Second Timothy 3 is one of the most amazing chapters in the Bible, for in it appears a startling description of the last days. If you read the chapter with a newspaper in hand you will be astonished at how well the Scripture text and today's headlines match. Now, 2 Timothy 3 is not a catalog of what Israel or Russia will be doing before Christ comes back. It is a description of what people will be like. Verse 1 describes the period by saying, "These will be dangerous times." They will be dangerous because of the death of love. There won't be love in that world.

Paul's orders to Timothy are included in the chapter, as are

God's orders to us. Verse 14 says, "But as for you, continue in what you have learned and have become convinced of, because you know those from whom you learned it....All Scripture is God-breathed and is useful for teaching, rebuking, correcting and training in righteousness." Paul is saying, "If you live in a world that is racing away from God's standards, you cannot afford to become like your environment—even a little!" There has always been a noticeable difference between lost people and God's people. Let's say, figuratively speaking, that the church is always ten miles closer to God than the world is. The problem is that as the world moves away from God, so does the church. Now we're still ten miles away from the marriages, the sexual standards, the hardness, the love of material things of the world, but as the world moves faster and faster away from God's standards, so do we! In a matter of five or ten years, we Christians will be where the lost were only a few years ago. But since we are still closer to God than the world is, we feel pretty good about it.

The rate of defection from God is accelerating. God's standard remains. God says, "You nevertheless. Continue to draw a line. Stand still. Don't move any further into your culture." True, you may feel pretty good about yourself if you compare yourself to what the world is doing, saying, and accepting, but that's not the measure. The measure is the God-breathed Scriptures of the Lord Himself. If you turn the light of God's Word on your life-style, you will see how far we have drifted! We dare not move any further into a secular mindset. What moving we do must be movement that leads us back to God's standard for love, for marriage, for honesty, for family—for all our relationships. Our environment is polluted and twisted. We dare not be like our environment. We must draw the line!

"**D**ad, can you fix this?" I hear that every once in a while. With my mechanical abilities, the best answer would probably be, "It's doubtful." But I will pull out my tool chest and give it a shot. One thing even *I* know—it is important to use the right tool. Let's say a wheel needs to be taken off a bike and brought to the bike shop for repair. Now, because I'm usually in a hurry, my first choice would be to reach for a hammer. A hammer gets the job done pretty quickly. It would also be my worst choice. I might be able to knock the tire off the bike, but the damage to the bike would hardly be worth it. Thus the hammer is quick but not particularly efficient. Some jobs require a wrench, and of course you have to find one the right size. Other jobs require a screwdriver, and here, too, you have to find the right kind of size.

Most fix-it missions require the right tool and plenty of patience. Fixing people is much the same. Without a proper tool and patience, you'll probably break what you are trying to fix. Someone you know is probably a candidate for...

## *Trouble-Free Repairs*

Second Timothy 4:2 says, "Preach the Word; be prepared in season and out of season; correct, rebuke and encourage—with great patience and careful instruction." Paul gives us in this verse three tools for our "toolbox," three tools we can use in fixing people. Now, I'm sure there's someone in your life who could use some work right now—right? Maybe you're married to such a person. perhaps the person who could use adjustment is a parent, or a child, or somebody in your church. How do you most effectively get that person to change? Well, you have to pick the right tool. Paul suggests three in 2 Timothy 4:2—rebuke, correction, and encouragement. To rebuke someone means to confront him with what he is doing wrong. Not long ago, one of our Youth For Christ staff people decided that she had to confront, to rebuke, as it were, a young girl who was a professing Christian but lived promiscuously and had a reputation with guys. The staff worker said, "I care enough to tell you what people are saying about you." The girl was shocked at what her reputation was. So we sometimes need the tool of rebuke.

Then there's the tool of correction. You don't just tell a person what he ought not to do. You suggest a better way to live—a "how-to-do-something-better."

Then there's the tool of encouragement. We need to apply the tool of correction by noticing the good in a person, praising what he is doing right, building up his confidence, showing your trust in him.

It is important to reach for the right tool. Don't encourage someone you should be rebuking, or rebuke someone who really needs encouragement. Use all three tools—but with great patience and careful instruction. Our natural tendency is to want quick results, so we drop bombs on people. We push them and they rebel—and don't change. We use the hammer because it will work quickly, but it smashes everything. We break what we are trying to fix.

When you rebuke or correct others are you patient with them? Are you too demanding? Do you escalate the rhetoric if you don't receive an immediate response? Help a person see himself as God sees him. Then back off. Allow time for the truth to sink in—give the person space to change without having to crawl. Use people-fixing tools with great patience. Then you won't break what you're trying to fix.

ot long ago I was in a meeting in a hotel room so chilly I was ready to put gloves on so that I could write my notes without shaking. Yet it was in the 90s outside. You've been there, too. It's hot outside, but the air conditioner is set one notch above high? Arctic—that was the setting. During the meeting various participants concerned wandered one by one to the box on the wall, just trying to see if there were some way to make the room less cold. We discovered that the controls were locked up. We couldn't get at them. So we called the front desk, and finally the maintenance man came and turned down the ice machine. Summer or winter, he's the person who decides what the temperature is. Well, so do we. We are responsible for...

## Climate Control

The Old Testament figure Nehemiah is one of the greatest models of leadership in all of the Bible. He was responsible for leading the monumental effort that resulted in the rebuilding of the wall of Jerusalem in fifty-two days! Not bad for a couple months of work. Nehemiah's story is told in the Bible book that bears his name. Nehemiah is governor of the province, and the wall has been completed. The people are trying to establish life in their rebuilt city. What is needed in order to establish a community is a climate of unselfishness, sharing, and cooperation. This climate Nehemiah supplies. For twelve years, Nehemiah told the people, "Neither I nor my brothers ate the food allotted to the governor. But the early governors—those preceding me—placed a heavy burden on the people and took forty shekels of silver from them in addition to the food and wine. Their assistants also lorded it over the people. But out of reverence for God I did not act like that. Instead, I devoted myself to the work on this wall. All my men were assembled there for work; we did not acquire any land" (5:14-16). Later, Nehemiah asserts that he "never demanded the food allotted to the governor, because the demands were heavy on these people" (v. 18*b*). That is leadership! Nehemiah was the man who set the pace. He led the way. He established a climate of sharing and giving—and the people followed.

The greatest responsibility of a leader is never written in his job description. It is the task of establishing a climate. Parents do it in their home. Teachers do it in their classrooms. Leaders do it in a church. Supervisors do it in an office or factory. Moreover, there is a sense in which we are *all* leaders, for we help to set the climate wherever we are. If you are in a position of influencing others, have you considered how the temperature feels where you are? What kind of climate are you establishing? It is not a matter of something you are doing consciously. It grows out of the sum total of your style, your values, your priorities, your pace. You establish it not so much by what you say as by how you live.

Is it tense around you? That may be the temperature you have set. Are people around you seeing a model of caring? Of unselfishness? Are you, like Nehemiah, pitching in on the job that needs to be done instead of just giving orders? Have you set a climate of respect for others by the way you speak to them and of them? Is there a climate of prayer around you? Have your co-workers "caught" that priority? Is there a climate of worry or trust? You are a leader. *You* control the climate, whether you realize it or not. Make your room feel as it would if Jesus were there. For if you are a Christian, He is in you.

**W**e kept two special mementos of our wedding. One was a piece of frozen wedding cake. The other was a tape of the ceremony. The tape was a much better idea than the cake. We ate the cake on our first wedding anniversary. You've heard of chocolate cake? This was more like *chalk* cake. It was terrible. But the tape—now, that was a great idea. In fact, even these many years later we often play it on our wedding anniversary. We relive that wonderful day when our marriage began.

Some couples have more elaborate ways of commemorating the day. For their twenty-fifth anniversary, they actually dust off the old wedding dress, reconvene what's left of the wedding party, and go through the ceremony again. However they do so, it is good for a couple to remember their wedding day. It's good to remember where it all began. The principle is true for any important relationship. A trip back to where it all began can rekindle the spark that once glowed brightly. That's why we need to be...

## *Remembering the Cross*

First Corinthians 11:23-26 has to do with remembrance. "For I received from the Lord what I also passed on to you: The Lord Jesus, on the night he was betrayed, took bread, and when he had given thanks, he broke it and said, 'This is my body, which is for you; do this in remembrance of me.' In the same way, after supper he took the cup, saying 'This cup is the new covenant in my blood; do this, whenever you drink it, in remembrance of me.' For whenever you eat this bread and drink this cup, you proclaim the

Lord's death until he comes." Have you heard those words before? Surely you have. They are familiar because they are the words Jesus used when He instituted the Lord's Supper. The disciples were to observe the Lord's Supper as a way of remembering Him and His cross. The Lord knew that believers would need often to return to the place where it all began.

The principle of remembrance is important. Yes, the observance of Holy Communion is established in 1 Corinthians 11:23-26, but so is the principle of frequently visiting the cross, for that is where we were bought. This return to the cross can happen at the Lord's Supper—surely it should happen there. But it can also happen in your bedroom or your study, as you let yourself wander mentally to the foot of your Lord's cross. You can visit the cross while you're driving, or when you are walking alone. At a time of great guilt you can visit the cross. At a time of great doubt and pain, you can visit the cross. Look into the eyes of the one who agonized under the weight of your sin. The hymn writer said,

> Beneath the cross of Jesus...
>> Mine eye at times can see
> The very dying form of One Who suffered there for me;
> And from my smitten heart with tears
> Two wonders I confess—
> The wonders of redeeming love
> And my unworthiness.*

At the cross you realize how serious is that sin you've been trying to justify. You realize how forgiven you are, how loved you are. You strip away the meetings and responsibilities and creeds and rules—and realize that Christianity boils down to two people: Jesus dying for you and you at the foot of His cross. It clarifies everything. Visit that sacred spot often. You will come away renewed.

*Elizabeth C. Clephane, 1830-1869.

**S**ome years ago we learned a way to make our vacation dollars stretch. We ordered ice water with our meals, instead of Coke. "Well, that's no big deal," you may say. Oh, yes, it is. If you have five in the family—as we do—you can save three or four dollars every time you eat out. Pretty soon you've got enough to eat another meal out! We do this throughout the year. So if you see us in a restaurant, don't be surprised if we order ice water with our meal.

Now frankly, I drink a good deal of ice water. So I try to persuade the waitress to leave a pitcher for us, though usually she won't. I want to save her steps, because we're going to clean up a lot of water. When I see her coming—well, I check my glass, and if it's partly full, I gulp the rest as fast as I can. I've seen people do the same with their coffee when they see the waitress approaching. It's called "empty it so it can be filled." The idea applies to our spiritual walk as well. It's the...

# Good News of an Empty Glass

Second Corinthians 12:7-10 gives us the testimony of an empty glass. Paul says, "To keep me from becoming conceited because of these surpassingly great revelations, there were given me a thorn in my flesh, a messenger of Satan, to torment me. Three times I pleaded with the Lord to take it away from me. But he said to me, 'My grace is sufficient for you, for my power is made perfect in weakness.' Therefore I will boast all the more gladly about my weaknesses, so that Christ's power may rest on me. That is why, for Christ's sake, I delight in weaknesses, in insults, in hardships, persecutions, in difficulties. For when I am weak, then I am strong." The Hutchcraft translation goes like this: "When I am empty, then I can be filled." You see, Paul was a man with great talent, great stamina, great knowledge, great influence. But some severe physical problem—his thorn—had him in its grip. In 2 Corinthians 12 he's saying, "The thorn hurts. It's tough to function with it. And I've got work to do. And here I am turning up empty." We say, "Oh, that's bad." He says, "No, that's good. Because when I'm empty, Christ can fill me. In those weak times there's just a little of me and a lot of Him!"

I can relate to Paul's experience, because I've been there—totally depleted, frustrated, hurt, disappointed, too tired to do what I had to do. Many times my radar is down, my emotions are spent. I can't even feel. And wouldn't you know it—there are people who need me then, and I have work to complete. I'm empty, but the Lord moves in gently. He says, "It's OK. There is not much of you left right now. Many times when there's a lot of you, Ron, there's too little of Me in what you do. But this time it will have to be all Me. Relax, and I'll fill you, strengthen you, take you outside your limitations into My unlimited resources." Those have been some of the sweetest, greatest victories of my life. And of yours. Look—if you've had it, don't give up. Open yourself up to being filled with Christ's strength. There's just a little of you, but now therecan be a lot of Him! If your glass is empty, that's good news! You are about to be filled with Jesus Christ.

**W**hen you've got a son who loves sports, you have to work hard to nurture his interest in music, for often the two interests don't go together. When our son was in the fourth grade we thought it was time to introduce him to a musical instrument.

"What instrument would you be interested in?" we asked him.

"Well, maybe the saxophone," he replied.

We didn't have a saxophone, or the money to buy one, but a friend called us and offered assistance. "I know you're interested in a saxophone," he said, "and I've found a classy, reconditioned instrument he might be able to use. It's all shined up and looks great—I'd like to make it available to you." Well, frankly, I wasn't sure how Doug and the saxophone would get along, until our friend handed it to him for a first try. I was expecting squawks and squeaks. But instead, out came notes loud and strong. It was great! Doug has been playing it loud and strong ever since. I looked at the saxophone the other day, and I realized that all believers are really just like that saxophone...

# Only an Instrument

In 2 Timothy 4:17 Paul talks about how God has played His tune through him. "But the Lord stood at my side and gave me strength, so that through me the message might be fully proclaimed and all the Gentiles might hear it." Paul is near the end of his life, and in this passage he's reflecting on his life's work. The two words he uses to characterize his relation to Christ as he works are the words *through* me. "The Lord, through me, is seeing that the message is proclaimed." Notice he doesn't say the message is being proclaimed "by me." No, he is saying, "Everything that is happening in my ministry is *through* me. The churches that have been established, the people who have come to Christ, the letters that are going to become part of the New Testament, and ultimately, the sermons that have been and will be preached—in all of this, I am just an instrument!"

That brings me back to my son's saxophone. It produces no music by itself. It's just lying there—a piece of shiny plumbing. It is only an instrument. It can play jazz, pop, gospel, even patriotic music. But the sax doesn't decide what it will play. The music is not *by* the sax but is *through* the sax. Without the musician playing it, it's useless. Shiny, yes, but only an instrument!

You and I are like that. God has designed each of us for a special purpose. We'll be useless if we try to play apart from Him. When we realize we are only instruments, good things will start to happen. We will relax, and we will discover that we can make a difference, because it isn't up to us.

Let the master musician pick you up and use you. Stop telling the Master what tune you should be playing. Let Him pick the tune. Give the credit where it belongs. Anything that happens as a result of my life or yours is not *by* you or *by* me, it is *through* you and *through* me! We can be surprised daily by what He will play through us. Daily we can wake up expectant that He will use us. We are instruments. We don't belong in the case. The Master Musician wants to play through our lives.

95

O n a recent vacation, our family had time to do some extra biking. There was a lake nearby, and it was fun to pedal around the lake. Well, sort of fun. The dowhill stretches were terrific. But guess what followed them—the uphill climbs. They were grueling—and sometimes painful. We quickly learned the trade off of...

# Downhill Thrill and Uphill Bill

My son reminded me, as we collapsed at the top of a particularly grueling hill, that the hill was "a lot like sin." "You know, Dad," he said, "we had a great time sailing down the hill, but the great feeling didn't last long. But it felt like it took most of the afternoon to get up the hill!" King David would agree with my son's testimony. He knew about the downhill thrill and the uphill bill. He spent his adulterous night with Bathsheba, and it was probably pleasurable. But then came the bill. When the Bible talks about the pleasures of sin it tacks on three words. The thrill of sin is only "for a season." The bill will surely follow. In Psalm 51:3, David steps forth after that sin and says, "I know my transgressions, and my sin is always before me." The pleasure wasn't always before him. His sin, his guilt, and the consequences of that sin were. They never went away—memories, painful ramifications, hurting relationships. You might ask, "Was it worth it, David? The downhill thrill?" He'd reply, "No way. There's too much pain for a short-lived pleasure. You pay much longer than you play."

You may be experiencing the downhill thrill of sin. It feels good. Seems like nothing's wrong. Maybe it's sexual sin, or maybe you've got a good situation you obtained through dishonesty. Maybe you're violating God's boundaries with your body, or you're partying with friends. Let me warn you—the uphill grind is coming. It always does! You can't stop it. It's a law of the universe. What you sow, you reap! If you sow your evil nature, you will reap destruction. That's what the Bible says. Right now you may be experiencing the good feeling sin gives. Maybe you have not yet reaped the consequences. It's easy to go with what you can see now. But the thrill isn't worth the price tag. This moment won't last. The loss, the pain, the consequences—they will last a lifetime. Take it from a tired biker—the uphill grind cancels out the downhill thrill.

**I** was at a Christian conference recently where the children's program included gymnastic instruction. I didn't get involved personally, because I really, well, my leotard doesn't fit anymore. But there were some kids there who were getting the hang of the forward rolls and backward rolls. There were also kids there who weren't getting the hang of it at all. Well, they paraded them all out one night for a little show. One girl raised her hands as she's supposed to, very gracefully, got in position to do a forward roll—and stayed there. She couldn't quite get the roll going. The instructor had to get behind her and push forward, again and again. It wasn't the little girl's muscles that were moving her, it was someone else's, but at the end she took a bow, just as if she had mastered the routine. She had the illusion she could do it, but unless someone was pushing her she was paralyzed. She was not so different from many of God's students I know. The real test is how you do...

## When No One Is Pushing

Philippians 2:12 contains Paul's commendation of some people who had truly learned their routines. "Therefore, my dear friends, as you have always obeyed—not only in my presence, but now much more in my absence—continue to work out your salvation with fear and trembling." Now this verse does not teach that you are saved by your good works. It teaches that good works are out-working in your daily life of the faith within your heart. Your faith works its way out so that people can see it. Significantly, Paul includes another point with the first. He says, "As you have always obeyed—not only in my presence, but now much more in my absence." As we would put it, "You don't just do it when I'm there, you do it when I'm not there." These people were following Christ consistently, not just when their leader was pushing. Many Christians who do the Christian "routine," do it as long as there is someone pushing. But that's a second-hand faith. What kind of a Christian are you when your boss is nowhere close? When your co-workers aren't watching? What happens when you're the only Christian in your service club, or your circle of friends? When your environment changes, does your faith change, too? If it does, it's a second-hand faith, and it just won't make it.

It's time you started to develop spiritual muscles of your own, whatever your age. Maybe you're too dependent on someone else to open up a Bible for you, or to keep you motivated and on track. You've got to develop your own discipline of time in the Word, of making Christ-honoring choices when nobody else is around to see, and of taking a stand on your own. It's risky to be God's person in this way, but it's such a good feeling when you stand for Christ and know you did it on your own, with only Him watching. Throw the crutches away and start doing some forward rolls on your own. Ask yourself, "What kind of a Christian am I when no one is pushing?" Start building spiritual muscles.

Even if your performance is a little clumsy, you're growing when you're rolling with your own spiritual muscles.

**E**very child loves a circus. And there's a child inside all of us that never grows up—and likes the circus. I've always been fascinated by those death-defying artists on the high trapeze. They leap with perfect poise from one trapeze to another until they end up safe on the platform, all the way across the arena from where they started. I guess that eventually you could get used to hanging onto a trapeze, and that you would feel comparatively secure as soon as you reached the next one. It's the time between trapezes that would bother me. We are most vulnerable when we're...

## *Living Between Trapezes*

Jeremiah 29 talks about life between the trapezes. At the time the chapter was written the Jews were in a temporary spot between two permanent spots. They had started out in Israel and they would end up back in Israel, but at the time Jeremiah 29 was written they were between trapezes, living in an in-between stage: captivity in Babylon. God's instructions to them—instructions to a people living between trapezes—must have been surprising to them. "Build houses and settle down; plant gardens and eat what they produce. Marry and have sons and daughters; find wives for your sons and give your daughters in marriage, so that they too may have sons and daughters. Increase in numbers there; do not decrease. Also, seek the peace and prosperity of the city to which I have carried you into exile. Pray to the Lord for it, because if it prospers, you too will prosper" (vv. 5-7). The message seems to be this: When you're in between, don't hold back! Live as if you'll be there for the rest of your life! God tells the exiles to build, settle, plant, increase, work for the good of that city. They are to improve things right where they are.

When you find yourself in an in-between place you may hear yourself saying, "Lord, this isn't where I want to be. I just want to get by until I get to my ultimate destination." Jeremiah 29:11 has an answer to that plea; " 'I know the plans I have for you,' declares the Lord, 'plans to prosper you and not to harm you, plans to give you hope and a future.' " You see, God's good plan for tomorrow comes from your living whole-heartedly today—in between trapezes. Today, maybe you are not where you want to be—you're between jobs, or you're in one that's just a stopgap. Or you're single—waiting, wanting to be married. Maybe you're living in a temporary situation or are looking for a breakthrough. Like the Jews of old, you are in an in-between place! Like them, God expects you to build where you are, to plant there, to increase your bounty, to improve the place. As you do, you will give God an attitude He can use to bring you His very best. Bloom where you are planted, be all you can be right where you are. It's the best way to safely reach that next trapeze.

**I** first remember hearing about it on Dick Clark's "American Bandstand." I suppose it was predictable that I would. Mostly teenagers watched the show, and they would have a big interest in the product, Clearasil. Like every kid, I saw my pimples as veritable mountains, so when I heard about Clearasil on "American Bandstand," I trotted out, got a tube—and another, and another—and hoped it would do the job. Today "American Bandstand" is gone, but Clearasil is still there, and kids are still buying it. As long as there are blemishes, we will be interested in a product or a person who is good at...

## *Removing the Blemishes*

What can be done to produce a woman who is without blemish? Ephesians 5:25-27 gives the answer. "Husbands, love your wives, just as Christ loved the church and gave himself up for her to make her holy, cleansing her by the washing with water, through the word, and to persent her to himself as a radiant church, without stain or wrinkle or any other blemish, but holy and blameless." The message is this: if a man loves a woman selflessly he will remove her blemishes. An unselfish husband is like an emotional Clearasil for the woman he's married to.

Every man marries an imperfect woman—and it's a good thing, because he's imperfect, too! Many things in the women in their lives frustrate those husbands. Maybe she nags, is too bossy, is not expressive enough, is too expressive. Maybe she talks too much, or is demanding, impatient, or preoccupied. whatever the blemishes are, you—as the Christ-figure in your family—have the power to change her, through your love, over a period of time. When a woman feels like royalty, she starts to act like it. You won't change her by nagging her, yelling at her, ignoring her, calling her names, attacking her, or criticizing her. When you do those things you will probably only delay change. You will change your wife the same way Christ changes us all—through patient, attentive, self-sacrificing love. Listen patiently to her words and her heart. Give her prime time—probably what you have the least of, so that's a sacrifice. Praise her, pitch in to help her with her responsibilities, give her surprises, court her, treat her like a queen in front of other people—a woman will blossom in the love of a man who puts her first. If you are concerned about your wife's emotional blemishes, don't buy her Clearasil—*be* her Clearasil.

**P**arental pride comes with a baby's birth certificate. New parents brag about their baby's first word, his first steps. They show off pictures of the baby to anyone who will look—and some who couldn't care less. And then they show off pictures of the growing child. If he's ever selected for a solo, or a starting position, or a part in something, or an award—his parents will be there with camera loaded. At some school concerts parents can be seen loaded down with tape recorders and video cameras. A parent has a special glow when his son or daughter makes him proud. It's supposed to work the other way, too. The Bible talks about...

# Parents Who Make Their Children Proud

Proverbs 17:6 says, "Children's children are a crown to the aged, and parents are the pride of their children." It doesn't say that children are the pride of their parents—it's the other way around! It says that parents are the pride of their children. Now that doesn't mean that a kid should run around showing off pictures of his mom and dad, or that he should take three rolls of pictures at some public event where Mom or Dad is on the platform. No, that's for parents. Parents tend to be proud of their children's *achievements*. Kids, on the other hand, tend to be proud of their parents' *character*. It's not so much *what* Mom and Dad do that make a young person proud, it's what they *are*. Our kids know the reality behind the image. They are proud if the reality, the real person they know is there day in and day out, when nobody's looking, is a person of quality and consistency in character.

What kind of a parent fulfills and makes his son or daughter proud? First of all, it's one who treats his children's friends with respect. You may or may not like all the choices of friends your children make, but you will make them proud when, as those friends come and go, you give them royal treatment. You want to have influence over your child's friends. You will win the right to comment as you let those friends be treated at your house as special persons.

Another way to be a parent your children can be proud of is to treat your children with respect when you are in public. Criticize and discipline privately. Praise, brag about, and build them up when you're in public.

You also can be a parent to be proud of when you treat your children's views with respect. Hear them out. Don't respond as though you know what they're going to say before they have said it. You might as well be telling them you don't value their opinions. Hear the whole paragraph, the whole page—not just the sentence. And respect their privacy.

A parent to be proud of has a positive attitude and is not a complainer, a whiner, or a critic. He is someone who respects his children's views but takes a stand for himself. My daughter's off to college. She's homesick. Someone says, "Why?" She says, "Because I miss talking to my best friend," "Who's that?" she's asked. "Oh, that's my mom." It may not be cool to advertise that your best friend is your mother, but my daughter has in her mother a parent to be proud of. God intends that your character and your attitude of respect and love be a source of pride to your son or daughter. I hope your child has a parent to be proud of!

**I**t was one of those ninety-degree special days. It was humid, and I was just finishing an eight-mile ride on my bike, feeling rather fit. Then I passed Tom, who was running all ten and a half miles around the lake. Tom does that every day. Nobody knows, nobody notices. But I'll assure you, he'll be in the headlines this year. Tom is one of the county's champion track stars. I yelled to him from my bike, "No time off for vacation?" He replied by reminding me that running is a twelve-month sport. Champions are not made the day of the race. They are made on...

# A Thousand Unsung Mornings

I've never understood people who get involved in a sport and settle for mediocrity. If you're going to do something, you ought to be all you can be. If that's true in sports, it is even more true when it comes to serving the King, the Lord Jesus Christ. Perhaps you look at "spiritual champions"—maybe someone you know, or someone you don't know but admire—and you want what they have. "I'd like to be used by God that way," you say. "I wish I could teach, or preach, or contribute music, or lead the congregation. I'd like to make a difference, to influence people for Christ the way they do." Let me tell you, you see them in a public setting—in the pulpit, on the radio, on television. You read the books they've written or hear them at a concert. But the ministry you see in a spiritual champion is because of something you don't see. Just like that championship runner chugging out the miles on those back roads, unnoticed, no one seeing, that's where the champion is built! Isaiah 50:4 says, "The Sovereign Lord has given me an instructed tongue, to know the word that sustains the weary." How does He do that? "He wakens me morning by morning, wakens my ear to listen like one being taught." "Morning by morning" there is a meeting with the Lord that no one sees. While others rest, the champion is in God's Word. He is on his knees. He doesn't go on spiritual binges and thereby gain some momentous spiritual insights. No, he is at it day after day, week after week, month after month. Finally, those days become years of accumulated time with the Lord. He speaks with a God-instructed tongue because he shows up for the class every morning. There's no man-made glory there—but there is the glory of Christ's personal presence.

I know that anything I've ever said for the Lord that has ever touched anyone has been because He touched me in private first, where no one else could see or hear. He wants to do that for you, for all His children. Do you want to be used greatly by your Lord? Then let Him teach each morning before you leave for the day. I see in that young track star a picture of any of us who would be God's champion, a winner being built on a thousand unsung mornings.

**M**y family and I were zipping along the interstate one day, when we saw a familiar bumper sticker. I noticed it, and I said, "Oh, that's nice," and began to pass. I could tell from behind the car that a mother and a child were riding in it, but the significance of the message on the bumper didn't hit me until I pulled alongside. Then, when I glanced over, it was obvious that the child was seriously retarded. That mother had a very heavy burden. I thought, *How does she cope with a responsibility like that?* Then I remembered her bumper sticker, and I had my answer. She knew how to...

# Handle a Heavy Load

Deuteronomy 33:25 relates directly to that bumper sticker. The words were familiar, but they may serve to remind you of something you need to keep in mind as you struggle with your own heavy load. The words on the bumper sticker read, "One day at a time." In Luke 9:23 Jesus tells us how to bear the cross of following Him. "If anyone would come after me, he must deny himself and take up his cross"—do you remember the next word?—"daily and follow me." Deuteronomy 33:25 contains a simple, profound, enlightening statement: "Your strength will equal your years." No, it doesn't say that. It says, "Your strength will equal your *days.*" God distributes strength to us in twenty-four-hour allotments. You have no strength for tomorrow today. Or for next week, or next month, or next year. Today you are facing what appears to be a mountain. You're saying, "I don't know how I'll get all this done." "I don't know how I'll make it through this crisis." "I don't know how I'll cope." The Lord says to you, "Take it 'one day at a time.' You don't have to conquer the mountain all at once. Don't try to handle that load. Take each day as I give it to you, in twenty-four-hour chunks."

When my wife, Karen, was ill with hepatitis for nine months —and I lost my right arm, my great strength, my great supporter—I tried for five weeks to be Mom on top of everything else. One day my pastor's wife said to me, "How did you manage five weeks without Karen?"

I said, "I didn't. I did thirty-five days." That's the only way we knew to do it.

You will never have a day when you do not have enough strength. God has promised. If the Lord sends you a hundred-pound day, you'll get a hundred pounds of His supernatural resources. Don't try to borrow tomorrow's trouble—you don't have the strength yet. But you *will*—when that day comes! Live as God designed you to live. Cope as He's equipped you to cope—in twenty-four-hour slices of life. If you do it one day at a time, you will make it through whatever challenges life places before you—for God's mercies are new every morning.